72 CONSUMMATE ARTS SECRETS OF THE SHAOLIN TEMPLE

COMPILED BY WU JIAMING

TRANSLATED BY ROU GANG

REVISED BY YANG YINRONG

FUJIAN SCIENCE AND
TECHNOLOGY PUBLISHING HOUSE

First Edition 1992

ISBN 7-5335-0486-0
Compited by Wu Jiaming
Translated by Rou Gang
Revised by Yang Yinrong
*
Published by Fujian Science and Technology Publishing Co. Ltd.
No. 27 Degui Lane Fuzhou 350001, Fujian, China
Distributed by China International Book Trading Corporation
35 Chegongzhuang Xilu, Beijing 100044, China
P. O. Box 399, Beijing, China
Printed in the People's Republic of China

Translator's Note

As the Chinese Martial Arts, especially Shaolin Wushu, are seldom interpreted into English, I even got none hope reference except the thin book "English-Chinese & Chinese-English Wushu Glossary". I cannot absolutely guarantee the accuracy of my translation. The most I can do is to assure the readers that my renderings are reasonable attempts. And the translations of the Book were sent to be vetted by my dear teacher Yang Yinrong, who gave me much help.

If these renderings contain some errors or mistakes that bring smiles to the lips of English-speaking people, I hope there will be smiles of compassion.

Translator : Rou Gang

Fuzhou Customs,
Winter 1990

Acknowledgements

During the translation of this work I have been extremely fortunate in being able to consult with Mr. Yang Yinrong, Mr. Chen Qiu, Lecturer Wang Chuncheng, Mr. Chen Junwan (General Secretary, Fujian Physical Culture & Sports Commission), Mr. Qi Ziyi (Principal and Chairman, Fuzhou Yat-sen Spare Time Foreign Language Institute), Mr. Li Zhixiong (Graduate student, Lancaster University, United Kingdom), Mr. Zheng Baixin (an interpretor of Fujian PCSC) and Mr. Wu Yaming. Without their help I should have found it far more difficult to translate this book.

Rou Gang, Fuzhou Customs

Compiler's Note

"Wushu worldwide originates from Shaolin"(Quoted from "Collection of Jian-Hu", Qing Dynasty). The temple won its fame from Wushu (Martial Arts)whereby the arts were entiled by its name. Shaolin Temple in the Song Mount. ,Henan Province,known as "the leading temple on earth",has fostered the development of Wushu and so enjoyed forever the prestige till now. Among all kinds of Wushu sects,Shaolin is the most long-standing, widest spreading and has been exerting the tremendous influence.

The Boxing Proverb runs: "No consecutive training when boxing, No gain when you are old". Shaolin Gongfu has long been one of the most important contents of Shaolin Wushu. It was regarded as the main weapon in health-building and self-protecting by the Shaolin Buddhists. It also serves as their fundamental skills for Seizing,Removing Bones, Pressing Acupoints,Light-Gongfu,etc. There have been many mysterious and fantastic legends of all ages about Shaolin Gongfu,for instance: "Gigantic Strength Outbursts From Hun Yuan Qi", "Drastic And Minute Golden-Clock Muscles Training", "Thirty-Six Rooms", "Seventy-Two

Skills", "Machine-Operated Wooden Men", "Ring For Martial Contests", "Plum-Blossom Stakes"and "Diagrams Of Boxing". The poem runs:

Inside the Wushu Bag seventy-two skills lie

Which are well-hidden, only Shaolin Arts so preciously implied.

Eighteen famous boxings have given the reason for why ,

And Eighteen Weapons are fully illustrated for try.

All fantastic ways of seizing under gentle breath, firm and ease.

With the Buddhists'blood, writing works were thus compiled,

Under the heaven with bloody training only heroes tie,

No pains, no gains, the universal truth runs right.

In this book , the seventy-two Shaolin skills are chosen and edited from both the traditional and the modern references of Chinese Shaolin Wushu. It contains exercise methods of one's body (the head, eyes, arms, elbows, fists, palms, fingers, back , abdomen, waist, kidneys, groins, legs, knees and feet.), Self-Hitting Arts, Falling-Pounce Arts, Dodging Arts, Stake Arts, Light-Gongfu, Qi Gong, Swimming Skill and all sects of internal and external Shaolin Gongfu. In addition to these contents, the book also enlists "Shaolin Temple Secret Recipe On Rescuing"and "Shaolin Wushu On Skeleton, Channels and Acupoints".

The references about Shaolin Wushu are oral or in manuscript. Due to the compiler's confined knowledge of making explanations and compilations, misinterpretations and mistakes are unavoidable.

Here I wish to thank readers for their incoming comments and suggestions after having put them into practice. These will always be welcome.

April, 1987.   .   **Wu Jiaming**

Contents

1

2

3

4

Four-Steps Arts

The First Step: Supporting the Sky and Lifting the Earth to Recuperrate the Sanjiao.

Body kept upright. Chest out and buttocks in. your eyes look straight forward and Your chin drops slightly. The left and right hands are crossed and the legs and arms closed up uprightly, so do the heels and toes (Fig 1-1). Gradually straighten your arms towards the left and right and raise your palms in a circle. While your hands reach to the top of head your ten crossed fingers then turn upward with the palms facing up. It seems as if you

Fig. 1-1

1

are supporting the massive goods. Your hands must be applied with force upward. The eyes look at the back of palms with neck stretching. The upper body slightly leans forward and bends down with your palms touching the ground, the lower the better. But you must still straighten your legs. Then the upper body slowly faces upward and you should apply force to press the arms to the left and the right. Your palms must be in a circle while doing so. And then return to keep an upright position. You had better take it easy (Fig. 1-2).

The Second Step: Five Kinds of Strain and Seven Kinds of Impairments to Look Back.

Keep your body upright. Your head slowly turns right and your eyes look straight backward and you try to peep at the left foot. While turning the head, your chest thrusts out. Stand still. Don't incline your shoulder. Your head turns to the front again (Fig. 1-3).

Slowly turn the head left. The eyes look straight backward and you try to peep at the right foot. And your head returns to the front. You must take it easy (Fig. 1-4).

The Third-Step: Push the Window and Look at the Moon to Drive away Heart-Fire.

Spread your legs apart in riding-horse stance and your chest thrusts out. Don't lean forward. Clench fists tightly waist-side. The palms face up with eyes looking straight forward (Fig. 1—5).

The left leg squats down and stretches out like spreading the rug. The left hand is in hook grasp towards the left and the right hand pushes the palm towards the right. Your body simultaneously turns to the right at the same time with the right palm. Keep the position of pushing window and look at the moon. The right leg squats down and stretches out.

2

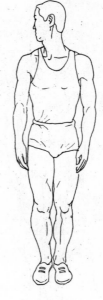

Fig. 1-2   Fig. 1-3

Your right hand is in hook grasp towards the right. The left hand pushes the palm towards the left and the body simultaneously turns to the left and your eyes look straight at the left palm. The left leg steps forward and returns to keep an upright position (Fig. 1—6).

The Fourth-Step: Clutching Nothing and Beating Nothing to Master the Vital Energy.

Spread your right and left legs apart in riding-horse stance and clench fists tightly at the waist-side. The right hand exerts force to thrust the fist and the fist up to the level of shoulders with the palm facing downward and the left fist remains the same. Your right fingers are

3

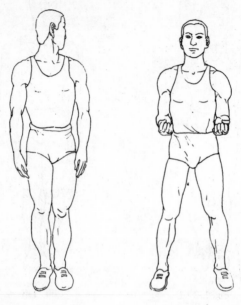

Fig. 1-4   Fig. 1-5

spreading and grasping backward and it seems as if they are clutching something. And then suddenly draw them back and return to be a tight fist at your waist-side. And then your left hand exerts force to thrust out the fist and keeps down the palm. While thrusting out the right fist your left fist gets to grasp backward and returns to the waist-side. Do it till you get exhausted. Finally draw the left foot back and keep it in upright position. The common saying goes: clutching nothing and beating nothing to acquire the Vital Energy (Fig. 1—7).

4

Fig. 1-6

Brief Introduction

1. Four-Steps Arts is one of the fundamental arts in the seventy-two consummate skills of internal and external Gongfu which were secretly handed down to the Shaolin Temple, Song Mount. , Henan Province. In comparison with Da Mo Eighteen Arhats't Hands and Yue Wumu's Eight-Steps Exercise they are different tunes rendered with equal skill.

2. In the First-Step Exercise, the Sanjiao (Triple Burner) refers to the Upper-jiao, the Middle-jiao and the Lower-jiao. It's a divisional line of one's body. The Upper-jiao (the upper portion of Body's Cavity) is located above the diaphragm, housing the Heart and the Lungs. The Mid-

5

dle-jiao (the middle portion of Body's Cavity) is located between the diaphragm and umbilicus of the body's cavity, housing the Spleen and the Stomach. The Lower-jiao (the lower portion of Body's Cavity) is located below umbilicus of the body's cavity, housing the Livers, the Kidneys, the Urinary Bladders and the Intestines. Sanjiao is the route wherein the Vital Energy and the Blood stream run. It holds responsible of the system of running all throughout the entire body. Therefore, to

Fig. 1-7

master the Shaolin Exercises, for instance, the Eighteen-Steps Arts and the Four-Steps Arts, etc, the trainees have to start with "Recuperating the Sanjiao".

3. Key to the Exercise: the Shaolin Master says that although the Four-Steps Exercise is quite short, while training one must keep away with all distracted thoughts and be calm enough so as to concentrate his mind and be easy to breathe in and out. Never can one hold his breath, or use up all his Vital Energy . Before bending down one had better take a deep breath. While Supporting the Sky with both hands one's fingers

6

must be crossed in order that his Energy can reach to the tips of the fingers. If possible, one had better lift his heels up. While one's palms are flating upon the earth, don't overexert one's force, otherwise it's harmful to his kidney. Don't be afraid of practising, never stop it half-way. Actions should be vigorously and slowly taken. Don't be too eager to take any quickening steps in the Exercise. In the progress of time, the more interest and diligence you take, the better you will achieve . By the way, the Exercise does not occupy much space and seems to be very simple. It will be quite effective in not too long a time and it contains a profound truth. After having succeeded one must avoid complacency. That is one of the basic skills to learn Wushu.

4. Note: "The Essence Of Shaolin Wushu", by the Great Master Da Mo, Shaolin Temple in the Song Mount, recorded that: "First, one had better find a fresh, clean and bright house. Don't face against the wind. Second, while it's heavily rainy, windy, stormy, thundering and the bad weather, one has to stop the exercise. Third, each day one can practise it for three times during the time Maau (Morning, 5 — 7), Wuu(Noon, 11 — 13), Yoou(Evening, 17 — 19). One should persevere in this training task assiduously. No need to increase or decrease the frequency. If one is busy he can practise it on an empty stomach during the Maau in the morning and when the sun is setting down one can do it during the Yoou. Anytime one may like to practise the "Wuu Training". Do remember: one must not eat anything just before training, otherwise the Vital Energy will be blocked up and he will hurt himself. Fourth, don't overexert oneself. Be in natural condition. Fifth, in the movement, don't take any medicine whenever one is ill or not, otherwise one's Vital Energy will stop transporting freely. Sixth, within the three months at start avoid

7

drinking wine and get rid of sexual intercourse. The weak must keep
them away for a longer time.

SECOND

Iron-Head Arts

At the beginning, one coils soft silks circling his head for more than ten rounds and wraps one or two iron-pieces outside, then bumps against the wall with his head several times only each day. While training, one had better lift his inner Vital Energy (Qi) to fill his brain. At the start, don't overexert force, for the skull is not hard enough and can easily be hurt. Gradually increase the harder-bumping times. More than one year later, after getting an initial result and decrease the silks to seven or eight rounds. Then after hundreds of days of practice, again decrease the silks to four or five rounds. One year later he may abandon the silk. Now he has reaped the second result. It's very uneasy for a trainee to bump straight against the wall. Step by step, one's head will be as hard as a brick. Now it surely means a success (Fig. 2).

Brief Introduction

1. Iron-Head Arts is one of the hard and external-strong arts in the seventy-two consummate skills of internal and external Gong-fu which

9

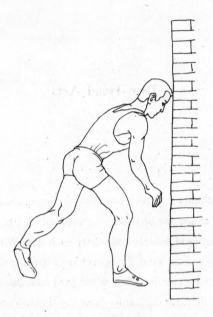

Fig. 2

the Shaolin Temple has inherited secretly, and it belongs to that of Yang
Gang character with internal-strong Qi. That is an exercise of one's
head.

2. The Wushu Illustration says; the head is the leader of the body
and is initially like the Heaven wherein the various Yangs converge. The
marrow-sea, which is the juncture of Yin and Yang, is governing the Vital Energy of the entire body. While it is in harmony with the Principle
of Yin and Yang, the Vital Energy of one's body must be in a good combination, otherwise the Vital Energy will deviate from normalcy. It is

10

stated in the Chinese medical book that, the head——— the marrow sea——— is the vital part of body. Eyes for looking, ears for listening, hands for working and feet for walking. They are all controlled and commanded by the head commander, therefore it's always taken to be the " Headquarters". In the Wushu poem the statement is: "Standing in the center, where the head so commands, the action of hands and feet immediately follows without the knowledge of others. "It is quoted above to stress the commanding position of the "Tou "(the head), and so does the Shaolin Wushu proverb says: "While one's head and neck are steady, his heart becomes calm and his Qi flows downward to Dantian". This indicates that one's head plays a very determinative role in controlling the actions of one's body. Thus its poem runs: "Like heaven the head is, the divinatory symbol belongs to Qian. Our actions, no matter whether we are standing straight, slanting, looking up and down, is in accordance with the principle of Nature. Whether we say yes or no is all originating from the head. What a great importance it is to assist erecting the Yin Yang Principle!"

3. In the Shaolin Wushu, the head was classified as the first role of all positions. Besides that, the emphasis is placed on the head which is the key organ of one's body connecting with the spirit, energy, sensitiveness and speed, etc. Illustrations are given to the head to show its special function of bumping in the actual combat. While making an attack upon the vital organs with the head, such as, the face, chest, ribs, abdomen and back, one may make his opponent lose the defending ability. In striking the method of head-bumping always predominates its special merit, for example, "Head Bumping against Golden Clock up on the Chest;" Phonenix's Nodding on the Face"; "Golden Cock Pecking on the Back".

11

All these skills can be used especially in the helpless condition when one's arms were unfortuntely embraced from the back by his enemy. These are really marvellous skills when you find ways to be out of danger. Boxing proverb goes: Such extensive strength is hidden in Lu Wei (draw back strength to the anus), and burst out from the neck. That's the drastic energy of the body. The "Headquarter" which launches an attack all at a sudden like lightening always offers an opportunity to turn defeat into victory. It is worthy for us to take Iron-Head Arts.

4. The head is mainly made up of the brain, skull and face. The brain contains the brain cavity. There are brains inside and cranial bone outside. The cranial bone consists of inner and outer compact bones and spongisa pressing from both sides. Outside, the cranial bone is wrapped up with solid fibre tissues, like a cap protecting the head, named in medicine: "galea aponeurotica". In the long-term exercise of "Iron-Head", the head structure and its function will be reconstructed, as gradually the skin is in active proliferation. The tenacity of the head skin and the elasticity of dermis will be much improved. Meanwhile, the frontal muscle will be well-developed, hardened and densified. In the long-run of bumping and stimulating, the gaelea aponeurotica and muscle tendon will eventually enhance a change from quantitative to qualitative. The galea oponeurotica and muscle tendon will become thicker and finer. The bone trabecula will then be arranged again. The osteogeretic function of cranial bone will be improved and it brings about the changes in the thickness of the inner and outer skull plates and in the improvement of bone tissues. It becomes very hard, thus improving the adaptability of the head to the outer force and strenthening the reacting ability of the head, thereby, we build up our protection skill and boxing techniques. It is said that

12

the Martial-Monk Miao Hui, who was the head of the South Shaolin Branch, was good at "Iron-Head Arts ", his nickname being "Iron-Head Buddhist of Shaolin Arhat". His head once bumped against a stone just as high as he was and crushed it into pieces, thus it could be seen that his " Iron-Head Arts" was so wonderful.

5. Key to the Exercise: the Shaolin Master says that the head of the man, who has achieved such an exercise, must be harder than a stone. Once the stone is being bumped by his head, it will surely be crushed, even an iron board will likely be deformed. He is second to none. If his head bumps against his opponent (There goes the common saying: "Bumping against Sheep's Head"), the opponent will die immediately. One must practise the skill assidously and make the best use of one's time to learn it. With tenderness in heart and calming down all Vital Energy and getting rid of all distracted thoughts one's brain will be as broad as Nature. Common saying goes: "One must first cultivate one's character before practising the skill. One will greatly succeed in it if only one does according to these methods. This Arts is a skill of defence. Comparing with other skills of combating, it's much beneficial for one to practise it. Moreover it is easier to learn. The Iron-Head Arts can be divided into three parts: the tectum of head, forehead and afterbrain. Although one must use one's external strength to build up one's physique, one must direct his strength and vital energy, through profound concentration, to his brain-house, and his Vital Energy (Qi) and "Shen" (Deity) will be in perfect harmony. If one just relys on the external strength without internal Qi, his Arts will be of inferior grade, even if he can achieve this Arts.

* Lift the Vital Energy: Here, the word "Lift" is abstract, refers to "inner-lifting"
or "to direct the Qi to Dantian".

Arhat Arts

There are several steps in doing this exercise. Shut your eyes while waking, massage them warmly with your thumbs fourteen times. With your eyes still kept closed, rub them (from left to upper-left, to upper-front, then to downward-right; from right to upper-right, to right and to downward-right; from downward-right to downward-front, to downward-left, and to the left) for seven rounds. This is just the same as the Arts of Opening and Closing Eyes in Boy's Eye Exercise. After rubbing all rounds, you need closing eyes for a quite while, then opening them wide suddenly. Use the back curve bone of thumbs to press closely the small acupoint (Zhuan-Zhu Acupoint) in the tip of the eye-brow for seventy-two times. Then rub the cheekbones with hands rotating around eardrops (Eardrop Acupoint) for thirty-six times, and rub the forehead on the reverse directions, beginning in the middle of the eye-brow toward the back of the head for seventy-two times (Do as the barber does by using fingers massages on the forehead). By so doing, you swallow into your mouth lots of saliva. Then paste a sheet of light green paper on the

15

windlamp which is burnt with sesame oil, and the flame of which must be small. Set it in the dark house. Stand before the light about two-zhan away (6. 6metres), cross your legs and sit on the bench with intense concentration of your will. Withholding the vital energy and watch the lamplight intently for about a quarter of an hour, then close your eyes, making the eyeballs rotate around as ever for thirty-six times and on the reverse direction (from the right to the left). Do it for thirty-six times. Then you widely open your eyes and watch the windlamp intently. A little while later, you return to close your eyes and practises the "Open-Close Eyes" Arts on the left and right and vice versa. Each night, practise it for about two hours. After three months you can deepen the colour of the windlamp paper a bit and the position can also be extended for about one or half metre away. Every day as you again deepen the lamppaper's colour from light green to deep green, the position can be removed from 6. 6 metres to 33 metres distance away. And the flame will be diminished from the size of a broad bean to the size of a soyabean, and the time of watching can be prolonged from two hours to four hours. Then yon can perceive anything in the darkness at night. Having done it assiduously without pause, you can distinguish who he is in the distance of 33 metres away. Now you are said to have been crowned with success (Fig. 3).

Brief Introduction

1. Arhat Arts is one of the internal arts in the seventy-two consummate skills of internal and external Gongfu which the Shaolin Temple has inherited secretly. It is a basic skill to train the visibility of one's eyesight.

16

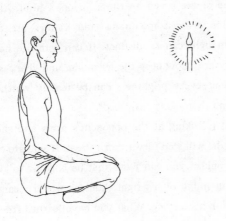

Fig. 3

2. The Wushu Guide states; the eyes, which are like the sun and the moon in the sky, are most honourable and respectable in the Wushu world, for the eye system is the convergence of all spirits. And whoever are coming from or going to, appearing or disppearing, leaping or hiding, they deeply influence us. While facing the opponents, the decisions through eye-sight must be made as to whether one is to be in the position of opening or closing, vainness or reality, highness or lowness. Then one can attack and defeat them thoroughly. An ancient philosopher stated that besides one's heart, the eyes and then the hands are most respectful. Therefore, the eyes are considered as a "Detector". The Boxing Proverb goes; "The fists are like meteors and the eyes like lightenings". "The eyes

17

are heart-seedling". "The eyes follow the hands and the steps follow the body". In the actual combat, the eyes must be the first, the bravery the second, the quick response the third. "In these statements, the eyes are described as the most important function not to be ignored. The poem runs: "The eyes are one of the seven apertures in one's head. All brightness can be seen, sights of vast mountains and valleys are entertained, minuteness or dim light can be distinct. It can estimate how high the clouds and the sky are, how deep the terminate and changes of Springs and sands do extend; every brightness can be readily watched, with all things carefully and thoroughly inspected".

3. Boxers say: Looking at the opponent's arms and shoulders one can judge whether he will step forward or retreat. If you are clear that he inclines his left shoulder, you can judge that he is going to kick with his right leg and the inclining of his right shoulder would means that he is going to hit you with his left leg. What you have learned from your eyes usually makes you feel at ease and use your discretion. To watch the upper body of the opponent with sharp eyes, one can immediately make a good decision of attacking or recessing, losing no chance to defeat the opponent. The statement says again: In the actual combat, one should have a thorough grasp of the situation and be quick of eyes and deft of hands. And one must judge the intention of the opponents with sharp-eyes and insert pins wherever there's a gap——make use of every bit of time or space to seize an opportunity to make a counterattack. It can be understood that when an opponent's shoulder inclines aside it would mean he is going to kick the other by his right leg. And while the opponent's right hand is going to be raised up, one must take precautions against his left fist. Though the situation is all the time changeable, one

18

should have a good idea of how things will stand. Watching the opponent's every mood and his intention, one yields a prompt response to the situation. Knowing perfectly well of the enemy's main force will lead you to strike at his weak points. Return to normal fight when you can make sure that you are the winner. As soon as you find your enemy's eyes to be looking at your left side, you should take precautions against his attacking from the left; If his eyes look at your right side, you should take precautions against his attacking from the right. While boxing with your close fist, your strength must be very strong. Having found your opponent's left leg on the front, you must take precautions against his right leg. Once the opponent has kicked the other by his back leg, you must take precautions against his further attacking. All these skills rely on the eye-watching. Experiences from the elders tell us that on the progress of a combat the function of eyes plays an active role in struggling for the initiative. The poem says: "Whenever one decides to attack or defend, one's eyes are detectors. In the actual combat two eye-balls must keep on incessantly rotating so as to follow your opponent's actions. Whatever you do depends on the circumstances. Having known the opponent's incoming way, you are invincible. "

4. In an action the visual sense is the sensibility on front guard. The eyes reflect every sight-seeing to the brain through the visual nerve. What they have seen doing will be distinguished by the brain which makes out due response through analysing and synthesizing. In the Wushu Proverb, the saying of "sharp-eyed and quick hands"actually points out that the "sharp-eyed"means a good ability of visual sense , coupled with a wide field of vision. During the long-term training of Arhat Arts, the eyes are being supplied with increasing nourishment and

19

their functions have been gramdually improving because of the movement of eyes muscle. The improvent of the partial blood circulation thus causing the new to superseds the old. By eyes watching, it is hopeful for one to concentrate his full spirit and becomes uninfluential and unfaltering with the result that his action and boxing ability will be greatly improved. Besides the Arhat Arts, there are the arts of Counting Leaf, Watching the Sun and Moon, Gazing At Fountain and Watching the Inflaming Tip of Joss Stick, But "their nature remains essentially the same despite all apparent changes." "Secrets Of Shaolin Wushu" written by Master Zhun Wo Zhai, 1915, CHINESE PUBLISHING HOUSE, states remarkably that "there are different points of eyes practising methods among the schools of Wushu. According to the theory of Guan Zhone School, while encountering the opponent, one had better look at his shoulders, and according to the theory of Luo School, one had better watch the opponent's chest; and according to the theory of North School, one must gaze at the weapon in the opponent's hand; and according to the theory of Chuan, Qing, Xiang, Chu Schools, one should glare at the opponent's eyes. All the above theories have their own advantages in each of the methods. We should not make improper comments abovt them, we should have a thorough comprehensive study of these subjects and learn from the strong points of others in order to offset our weakness. So the point of difference between the Shaolin Wushu from all others'and above others' is that it pays great attention to the internal exercise as well as its inner technique. What is the internal Gong? That is to relieve life from death, remain fully awake and conscious. The eyes are like lion's, as sharp as those of an eagle. Its curiousness is unimaginable. What one's eyes are gazing at in the Shaolin Wushu is the opponent's eyes. Having a good command of this arts, one will be able to be on the watch for opponent's hands and his weapons at the same time. The beginner can not be proficient in it". The poem also runs: "How wonderful and true the eye-method of Shaolin Wushu is! The eyes are forerunners as well as directors of hands and feet and tell you the truth. Defeating the enemy with a pair of eyes, which are the sun and the moon of ours, will lead us to conquer the whole world as well. With the eyes you can be as brave as a lion, and as vigour as an eagle. One can make decisions by judging the opponent's eyes, and naturely one can be on the watch for the opponent's hands and weapons and have a good command of the Exercise".

5. Key to the Exercise: the Shaolin Master says that if you can assiduously learn it, you are bound to achieve this art. Of course, there exist fellows who can see things in the dark, but our purpose of exercise on eyes is a necessary step for one to learn the Arts of perceiving minute things in the dark. If you can distinguish the things in the dark, should you be said to have achieved good results in the exercise. Then you can not only walk at night, but also swim with your opening eyes in the water. The common saying goes "If you perfect your 'jujube'(the symbol of eyes), you can gain extra advantage in actual combat. "Each day, before dinner you had better take a little sheep liver, which can help to increase the internal energy of your vision or eye-sight.

Iron-Arms Arts

At first one can strike slightly the house-pillar with his arms several times a day. Thereafter, strike strongly with his arms against it. The arms will become hard. Then one can strike a tree-trunk with his arms instead. As its surface is so rough, he may be painful and his arms will be swollen. After one year one can strike a stone instead of the tree-trunk. He may first strike a flat and smooth stone with his arms, then a rough stone instead. If he is able to strike a stone and crush it with his arms, he will be considered to have attained the achievement. Now one's arms are completely as solid as iron and stone. If he strikes an opponent with his arms, he may break the opponent's sinews and bones. Even if one faces an opponent's broadsword or a stick, he is able to break them too. Even though one is bare-handed, he will win the combat at ease (Fig. 4).

Brief Introduction

1. Iron-Arm Arts is one of the hard and external-strong arts in the

Fig. 4

seventy-two consummate skills of internal and external Gongfu which
the Shaolin Temple has inherited secretly. It belongs to that of Yang
Gang character. This is a specific exercise of one's arms.

2. The Wushu Guide says: one's arms are gates and doors of his
body. One should close them, not to leave them open. If they are open,
one may neglect his fighting will, and an opponent will snap at him by
thrusting his fists or palms. And it will be rather difficult for one to protect himself. One must direct his Vital Energy to his arms. While the
arms are being raised up, the Vital Energy will naturally follow

23

them. While putting down the arms, the Vital Energy will naturally trace them. While opening the arms, one's body should turn with them. Don't let them alone. The Wushu proverb goes: "The actions of arms must be connected with the will and Vital Energy. " "Twisting waist, extending shoulder and bending arms". These statements show the highly important function of the arms in the Shaolin Wushu.

3. In the Shaolin Boxing, one can see that the boxers usually make use of the side of radius and ulna of his arms to attack or defend, for instance, to parry one's arm from inside to outside, to press one's arm from front to forward, to sink one's arm from up to down, to block one's arm from down to upward, etc. The method of attacking and defending each other is called Qiang Shou (Hands race to control). The rule of Qiang Shou is that: One fends off, the other seizes; one seizes, the other defends; one defends, the other wrests; one wrests, the other seperates; one seperates, the other joins; one joins, the other changes; one changes, the other puts up; one puts up, the other goes through; one goes through, the other draws back; after drawing hands back then turns to fend off. Again and again, in the course of practising endless possible changes of Qiang Shou may take place. In the Shaolin Wushu, one's arms are required to take a curved posture, regardless of defending or attacking. There remains plenty room for manoeuvre and it's favourable for the great changes of hand techniques.

4. In the practice of Iron-Arms Arts there are specific parts of the body: they include the shoulder back (deltoid muscle, infraspinous muscle), the postarm (biceps muscle of arms, brachial triceps muscle), the forearms (brachioradial muscle radial flexor muscle of wrist, long palmar muscle, ulner extensor muscle of wrist, etc.), the elbow (elbow

muscle) and the wrist (muscle tendon). After practising the Iron-Arms Arts, one's arms will be stronger and bigger, their muscle will be full-grown; their skeleton will be solid; their ligament will be flexible, tough and tensible. The mastery of Iron Arms Arts will strengthen one's adapability to circumstances. At the same time one will gradually get to know that the strong strength of the arms muscle is essential for offering resistence. By practising the Iron-Arms Arts, one can strengthen the explosive force of his upper limbs to make his arms tough, tensible and flexible, and to enable him to deal with cases skillfully. It means that one can gradually reach to the standard of Shaolin Wushu in the case of combating after attaining the achievement of "Mastering the vital energy by internal training, and strengthening the health through external practice". And one's goal of success will be that: as soon as one strikes with his arms against the iron-pillar, he will break it immediately. In the combat the Iron-Arms Arts will play the powerful role in attacking and defending.

5. Key to the Exercise: the Shaolin Master says that this Gongfu is not only simple and effective for one to practise but also easy to achieve. During the first year of practising, one will get an initial result. If one keeps on practising this Arts, he can come to a successful end.

FIFTH

Double-Key Arts

First, one strikes his forearms against each other and it causes unbearable pain. Later on, one may feel no pain for his arms muscle is becoming hard. While one's arms strike against each other, there will be a sound of a crash. This is the first step. Then, strike the wrists, fists, palms, two fingers and a single finger against each other. One can not be said to have achieved the second result until he has heard the sound of a crash. And then one is to go to strike his arms against his forelegs (the right and left knees must be raised) until the skin becomes soft and flexible, he has accomplished a great success (Fig. 5).

Brief Introduction

1. Double-Key Arts is one of the hard and external-strong arts in the seventy-two consummate skills of internal and external Gongfu which the Shaolin Temple has inherited secretly. It belongs to that of Yang Gang character. This is a specific exercise of one's arms.

2. Key to the Exercise: the Shaolin Master says that anyone, who

26

Fig. 5

has achieved this Arts, can break a broadsword barehanded. If his arms cross each other they are just like a hand hay cutter. And it's quite easy to practise this Arts.

Pot Lifting Arts

Use a two-ear small pot as an implement, tie a short cord to its both ears. And then take one-meter-long cotton cord, one end being tied to the central point of the cord and the other end to a round log which is one foot and two inches in circumference and suitable for one to hold it. The log is preferably made of jujube tree. It must be rough, and you should drill a hole at the centre of the log. Let the cord's end go through and tightly tie to the log. The weight of the pot is about six or seven catties, being filled with three catties of iron-sand. At the start its weight can not exceed ten catties. While training, one is to be in riding-horse stance to erect his upper body with his hands holding the log in front and lifting the pot in midair till his elbows are up to his shoulders level. At this moment one is to straighten his forearms and slightly lean forward with his palms facing out. After lifting up the pot, he has to wait until it stops swinging. Then his hands hold both ends of the log tightly and make the log gradually rotate inward. Thus the cotton cord is slowly spinned to the central part of the round log and the pot is slowly raised up to the chest level. After a while one slowly puts down the pot. One may practise this Arts for about thirty times each morning and evening. After three months, add 3 taels of sand into the pot. In the course of training, add the weight of the sand for five times. After three months, half a catty of sand is to be added. Later on, one can add half a catty of iron-sand every three months. The weight must be increased every three months, till the total weight of pot is about 30 catties. By this time his strength to withstand holding fast a thing in midair will be ex-

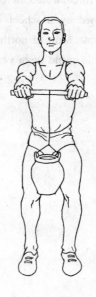

Fig. 6

ceedingly tough. Satisfactory effects will result only when one stands at a high stake to make practice with a cotton cord of two metre long (Fig. 6).

Brief Introduction

1. Pot Lifting Arts is one of the hard and external-strong arts in the seventy-two consummate skills of internal and external Gongfu which the Shaolin Temple has inherited secretly. That is a specific exercise of one's arm. It belongs to that of Yang Gang character.

2. Key to the Exercise: the Shaolin Master says that the method of

arms lifting-force, which includes the practice of holding-force, is adopted and learned by a school of disciples taught by the master in the Shaolin Temple. Most of northerners practise this art. From beginning to end one should spend three years to accomplish it.

SEVENTH

Key-Stone Arts

The appearance of the stone key is just like that of a copper key, with a spring and a shell but without a key hole. It is made of granite stone or green stone. The weight of the smaller one is about twenty catties and the bigger ones vary in weight from 60 to 70 catties. At the start one just practises lifting and holding arts. First, hold the spring with one hand and lift the stone key high up to reach the front chest and turn the wrist to raise it up and down several times in order to practise one's arm force. Then forward hold the stone-key, lifting from the lower to the upper or to the sideway until the arms are level with shoulders in order to practise the arms' force to withstand suspending. After getting this basic skill, one can go on practising the Arts of overturning-catching and coiling-waist. It refers to that of exerting force to hold the spring of the stone key, lift it up and then let it to slip out of the hand to make an overturn two or three times in midair and at last catch it. The number of overturning and catching depends on one's arms' force. At first, it is not advisable to lift it too many times. After getting acquainted with it, prac-

31

tice will make the Arts perfect. Satisfactory effects will eventually be taken when one raises his hand to catch the key spring and as the keystone turns to one's face, one is to try to seize the chance to overturn it continuously. After doing it skillfully, one can shift to practise the side-overturning Arts. After that, one can further practise to carry the stone key on the fist. Throw it up. While it falls, carry it on the fist for a moment. Then let go the stone key and at the same moment turn to catch its spring. Do this exercise again and again. At first one can use his fist to support the stone, then use the of his hand, his forearms, elbows and fingers. The method of practice remains the same. After having practised to support the stone key with the fist thoroughly, one may come to learn the "Back-Flower". It is divided into left and right in direction. The right "Back-Flower" requires to lift the stone-key with the right hand, throwing it from the right back part of the waist to the rear of the left shoulder, slightly turning one's body to the left, and catching it from the front position of the left shoulder and the left "Back-Flower" is to practise it on the reverse direction. Don't overexert force while practising the Arts of "Back-Flower". Take good care of one's waist and ribs. Due to the lack of vigilance, one may encounter serious injury. Where there are one's hands, there go one's eyes. The second stage is to continue to learn Coiling-Waist. It is also divided into left and right. The right Coiling-Waist requires to lift the stone key with the right hand from the back of the right waist and throw it upward to pass under the armpit and then turn the body to the left to catch the stone key. The left Coiling Waist is done on the reverse direction. There are other methods of practising Back-Flower—— "Backward Lifting and Catching" and "Coiling-Waist Backward Lifting And Catching". One can combine two methods into

32

one according to one's interest and condition. After finishing the methods of these drills, one can use heavier stone keys instead for further practising. The weight varies from 20 to 60 catties. If one makes the above practice without difficulty, he will be able to hold the weight of 300 catties with his single arm. Practise it with two hands by turns. It is very easy and is a speedy way for one to learn it. This Arts will be accomplished in about two years (Fig. 7).

Fig. 7

Brief Introduction

1. Stone-Key Arts is one of the hard and external-strong arts in the seventy-two superb skills of internal and external Gongfu which the Shaolin Temple has inherited secretly. It belongs to that of Yang Gang energy. This is a specific exercise of one's arms.

2. Stone-Key is one of the instruments in martial arts, which is made of stone in which a hole is chiseled. Its appearance is just like an ordinary Chinese old trunk. It's said, long, long ago, that in the regions of rivers and lakes in the South Yangtze River, there lived many fishermen year in year out. When they came across pirates or robbers, they used boatplanks as a weapon. Afterwards they found that the boat planks did not work well and gradually they utilized the wooden-key instead. The stone-key was developed from the wooden key.

3. Key to the Exercise: the Shaolin Master says that this is to drill one's lifting energy. Its effect is not weaker than that of the Iron-Bag Arts.

Iron-Bag Arts

First, get some very thick cloths to be mended together and sew a square bag, in which iron-sand is filled. The weight of a smaller bag is about ten catties while the weight of the larger ones may vary from 40 to 50 catties according to the energy and arts of drillers whenever necessary. While training two persons stand sideways to sideways, the distance between them being about 3.3 metres. One of them holds the centre of the bag with his right hand, lifting it up to his shoulder blade and throwing it out from the right to another's front. While catching sight of the flying bag to his front, the partner slants his body to let go the bag to fly to the position of his left shoulder blade, then quickly stretch out his right hand to catch it. While catching, he has to hold the center of the bag and stands steadily. If only catching the edge of the bag, he won't be able to handle it with his fingers at ease. After catching it, don't stop, and throw it back (at once) to his partner without delay, and his partner catches it in the same way. Then throw the iron sand bag to and fro each other for more than ten times. Then change the direction and do the practice with

35

the left hand. Both of them must be equally tall and equivalent in strength, otherwise, there will be many disadvantages for them to throw the bag against each other. For instance, the stronger may exert force vigerously and it's burdensome for the weaker to catch it. Even if the latter does catch it, he will have to bend his body to follow the bag in rotation and might hurt himself. At the beginning to do practice, one should not go in for making ambitious projects to hold the heavy bag. If one can lift 20 catties of things, he had better take 10 catties of iron sand bag to make practice. One reason is that to throw the bag requires mightier strength than to lift it. Another reason is that drilling this Arts requires gradual improving. After throwing the ten catties iron sand bag for three months, the weight of the iron sand bag can be added by one or two catties. The weight of iron sand bag is to be increased gradually every three months till it comes up to 50/60 catties. From A to Z, one may have to spend four or five years to finish practising this Arts(Fig. 8).

Brief Introduction

    1. Iron-Bag Arts is one of the hard and external-strong arts in the seventy-two consummate skills of internal and external Gongfu which the Shaolin Temple has inherited secretly. It belongs to training one's muscular energy. That is a specific exercise of one's arms.

    2. It's very helpful to practise the Iron-Bag Arts. It does play an important role in Tumbling Boxing and Fighting of the Shaolin Wushu. With this arts, one increase the strength of fingers, arms and the toughness of both the fists and the arms. There are some advantages about the Iron Bag Arts. (1)The bag is very handy. (2)It's quite simple to make it and it costs only a little money. (3)To practise this arts doesn't occupy

36

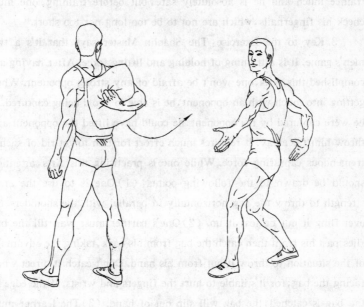

Fig. 8

any spacious place. One can even practise it in a cow's sleeping spot.
(This is a common characteristic of the Shaolin Wushu. It is known as

"To practise this Arts within a limited space that it's large enough to house a cow"). (4)It does not require anything hanging nor does it need to be subjected to be done in a house. It can be drilled by pairs and might as well be played by lots of people. It is enjoyful if one can attain the training achievement. (6) Unlike stone-keys, this Arts doesn't hurt a trainee much and he is absolutely safe, but before training, one must check his fingernails, which are not to be too long nor too short.

3. Key to the Exercise: The Shaolin Master says that it's a two men's game. It is a training of holding and lifting force. After having accomplished this Arts, one won't be afraid of any strong opponent. When getting into touch with an opponent, he is able to avoid being captured. If he were captured by his opponent, he could have lifted the opponent and throw him far away. It requires much effort for him to get rid of such a tremendous capturing force. While one is practising this Arts, attention should be drawn to the following points: (1) One is to use the arms strength to throw the bag horizontally in parallel with the shoulders. Never fling it out or toss it up. (2) One's partner must wait till the bag flies past his front then catch the bag from his back, taking the advantage of the situation to throw it out from his hand. Don't catch it direct when facing the bag, for it's liable to hurt the fingers and wrists. If the edge of the bag is catched, the bag will slip out of hand. (3) The learner must stand steadily on his leg no matter how and where he stands, otherwise he may decrease the throwing force due to his unsteady steps. The catcher should also stand steadily or he may be swayed by the bag. The trainee should pay close attention to the above three points. Besides these points, the learner should not rigidly adhere to the traditional routine!

Thousand-Catties Floodgate Arts

At the start, one can practise the Arts barehanded in the riding-horse stance. Raise both hands up to the top of his head with fingernails turning down and palms up. The position is just like that of Supporting the Sky and Lifting the Earth to Recuperate the Sanjiao in the Eight-Step Arts of Yue Wu-Mu (well known hero in the Song Dynasty). It is an exercise of lifting force. After three months, one may begin lifting the stone block. At first, its weight is about 20 to 30 catties. Thereafter, one is to increase gradually the weight of the stone block up to 200 catties and keep on lifting it for more than half an hour each time, neither gasping nor sweating. Then practises it with floodgate stone. The installation of a floodgate is that of setting up two large wooden pillars, standing side by side, and that meach pillar a deep trough road is chiseled and two trough roads are to face each other. Besides these, one prepares a few long stone-slabs, each of which varies from 30 to 200 catties. At first, one fixes both ends of a 200 catties stone-slab into the two trough roads, then tie the middle of the stone slab with a rope and pulls it up to a height of 4

39

feet above the ground. Then fasten the rope fast so as not to let the stone slab slip down. The learner can squat down in the middle between the two trough roads and lift the stone slab up and support it with his hands. After having trained for a few days, one can add a lightest stoneslab inside the troughs. And several days later, take away the lightest stoneslab and use a heavier one instead. Step by step, add the stone-slab in the same way. If one can lift up a 500 catties stone-slab, he will be able to resist a hundred opponents. Should he be a born strong person, he might be able to lift up a weight of 1,000 catties. The common saying that a mere swaying of both arms may produce 1,000 catties of force just refers to this Arts. The training time can be arranged according to one's choice (Fig. 9).

Brief Introduction

1. Thousand-Catties Floodgate Arts is one of the hard and external-strong arts in the seventy-two consummate skills of internal and external Gongfu which the Shaolin Temple has inherited secretly. It belongs to that of Yang Gang character. This is a specific exercise of the arms and the other parts of the body.

2. There is difference between Thousand-Catties Floodgate Arts and Weight Lifting. The former is one of the traditional exercise methods in the Shaolin Wushu, whereas the latter is one of the items of physical sports. Generally, to practise the former is more difficult, for it's the basic exercise of health-building and the foundation of Wushu. It is different from the Stone-Key Arts, which lays particular emphasis on the lifting force of arms.

3. Key to the Exercise: the Shaolin Master says that outwardly, the

40

Arts is the practice of lifting and supporting force with palms and fingers; actually it's the training of the three parts of the body. Having achieved this Arts, not only will one astonish all because of his arms' force, but also have great power all over his body. Evidently, his muscles will be hard and his strength will be steady. The training process is very simple and stiff. And it's very efficient for the born strong person to practise it. If the short and weak person

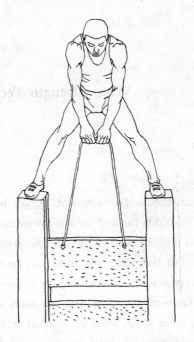

Fig. 9

practised it, he would have difficulty in making progress. The majority of northerners practise this Arts. This is a most effective method to strengthen one's force.

41

Whip-Strength Technique

First, choose the method of "Upper-Bar", i. e. set one's forearms flat on a wooden bar and press it down, let one's body rise up gradually in midair until his waist is up to the le vel of the wooden-bar, then slowly lower his body. The high table can be used instead of the wooden bars. Every morning and evening, try to practise this skill. One raises and lowers his body for more than ten times and gradually increases the training times. If his arms are swollen or painful, they can be washed with liquid medicine. After about one year's practising, one's forearms will be strong enough. Then, practise it with a bamboo-stand. The structure of the bamboo-stand is made by driving four wooden stakes into the ground to shape a square, just like the feet of a table. Then, two pieces of large bamboo are to be bound to both the left and right ends of the stake-tops. Later on both ends of four or five bamboos poles are fastened with soft ropes to the large bamboos horizontally so as to look like a table-top. The learner is in a riding-horse stance and sets his forearms on the horizontal bamboos poles and presses his forearms down with sudden force

Fig. 10

for about a quarter of an hour. Take a rest before another practising. At first, the bamboo tabletop may only be pressed down for about $1-2$ inches. Another bamboo pole can be added under each horizontal bamboo pole. Afterward they can be pressed down for about $6-7$ inches. As in the previous method, a third piece of bamboo pole can be added under the second bamboo pole again. By adding successively like this, from one bamboo pole to more than ten bamboo poles. One can achieve the Arts after he can press more than ten bamboo poles down for about $6-7$ inches. From beginning to end, one should spend three or four years.-

43

When the skill is achieved, one can crush a stone if one's forearms press on it (Fig. 10).

Brief Introduction

1. Whip-Strength Technique is one of the hard and external-strong arts in the seventy-two consummate skills of internal and external Gong-fu which the Shaolin Temple has inherited secretly. It belongs to that of Yang Gang character. This is a specific exercise of the arms.

2. Key to the Exercise : The Shaolin Master says that Whip-Strength Technique is a special exercise to train the pressing force of the fore-arms. It is a bit similar to that of the Iron-Arms and Separating Water Arts. But it lays emphasises on the pressing force. Not necessary to use the strength of beating and fighting. After accomplishment one can defeat his opponent and break his opponent's bones. And one's arms are not easily be injured by a broadsword, for his forearms are just like a pair of iron-whips, called, "Whip-Strength". The learner must be careful of his own behaviors, for he may accidently injure the others.

ELEVENTH

Separating Water Arts

First, bury a row of dozens of bamboos which are tied with iron-chains in the upper and lower ends, place them close together one by one tightly like a bamboo-wall with no crevice. The learner first uses his closed palms and tries his best to insert them into the crevice between the two middle bamboos. The bamboo is pliable and springy. Although there is no crevice between two bamboos, it may be opened if one exerts to separate them. After inserting his hands into the bamboo wall, he must exert his arms force to keep the bamboos apart. At the start there is just a small crevice, but if one keeps on practising, he will gradually be able to make the crevice open like a door, through which one can come in and go out. Now, bury over ten to tens of big bamboos on both sides to make a big bamboo wall like before. If one can also separate and close the bamboos at will, he can be said to have reaped the first fruit. It is clear that, if a bamboo is added to the row, one is required to have more than 100 catties of force to separate the bamboos. With 30 large bamboos to form a wall, one will need to have at least thousands of catties of power in his

arms. After that, build
a wall by piling up fine
sand to form a wall or
making use of an earth
wall in the country-
side, and insert one's
arms into it and sepa-
rate it to the left and
right. Satisfactory ef-
fects will result from it
only when one can
separate the sand with
his arms at ease and
the sand does not fly
about (Fig. 11).

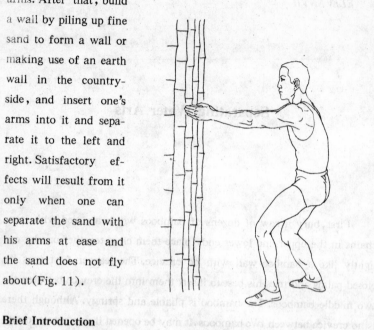

Fig. 11

Brief Introduction

　　1. Separating Wa-
ter Arts is one of the
hard and external-strong arts in the seventy-two consummate skills of
internal and external Gongfu which the Shaolin Temple has secretly inherited. It belongs to that of Yang Gang character. This is a specific exercise of one's arms.

　　2. Key to the Exercise: The Shaolin Master says: there are tech-
niques of Separating Mountain, Palms of Separating Water in the
Wushu. They are all originated from this Exercise. The Power in this
Arts is completely gathered in the arms with the help of the palms. It is

46

really the function of hardness and softness moving in harmony. After having accomplished it ,one can keep away thousands of opponents and his actions are surging with great momentum.

TWELFTH

Jade-Belt Arts

Stand under a tree, embrace it with both arms, with both hands grasped tightly. Then, try your best to pull it up. Don't stop the practice until you are completely exhausted each time. After one or two years of practice, your strength of arms will get to be stronger and stronger. Being embraced and given a shake, the tree trunk will seem to be broken and the leaves and twigs will fall down with rusting. This is just the initial result. When you can pull up the tree completely, you can then attempt to embrace a stone drum weighing about 4 to 5 hundred catties. A stone drum is not easy to be embraced because it's very heavy and its surface is smooth. You may try to embrace and lift a stone drum up just for the purpose of improving your fastening power. After making practice for one or two years you can embrace the stone drum and walk around at will. Now you have accomplished this Arts because your embracing power is amazing (Fig. 12).

48

Brief Introduction

1. Jade-Belt Exercise, also called "Buddha Maitreya Arts", is one of the hard and internal-strong arts in the seventy-two consummate skills of internal and external Gong-fu which the Shaolin Temple has inherited secretly. It belongs to that of Yang Gang character and of the Vital Energy of Yin Rou. This is a specific exercise of the arms.

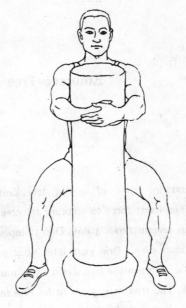

Fig. 12

2. Key to the Exercise: The Shaolin Master says that the embracing method places emphasis on the arms force. And, it is also called Qian Kun Circle, a very simple exercise. It was said that a blind boy, who wanted to learn the Wushu, came across Chao Yun, a Buddhist monk, by whom the boy was taught this practising method. Later the blind boy defeated his opponents and won fame for his skill.

Embrace-Tree Arts

Stand in front of a big tree. Embrace its trunk with both hands. Then exert force to embrace the tree tightly and try your best to pull it up several times a day. Don't stop until you are completely exhausted each time. One year later your arms will be strong enough. When you embrace the tree again , you must be able to give a shake to the trunk. The tree may seem to be broken and its rustling leaves and twigs are seemed to be falling down . Now you have reaped the first fruit . At the end of the second year when the tree is to be embraced , it will turn withered . Now your chest and abdomen become as solid as iron or stone . You have reaped the second fruit . Keep on practising this Arts for three years, you will be able to pull up the tree completely. Now you have accomplished this Arts (Fig. 13).

Brief Introduction

1. Embrace-Tree Arts, also called "Buddha Maitreya Arts" , is one of the hard and external-strong arts in the seventy-two consummate skills

50

Fig. 13

of internal and external Gong-fu which the Shaolin Temple has inherited secretly. It belongs to that of Yang Gang character and of the technique of directing the Vital Energy of internal Gongfu. This is an exercise of the arms and chest. It is similar to that of the Jade-Belt Arts.

　　2. During the years of Kai Huang in the reign of Wen Emperor in the Sui Dynasty (A. D. 581-618), it was said that there was a buddhist monk, called Wen Zhao, who excelled at this "Embracing -Tree Arts"· He was able to embrace an old bell, 800 catties in weight, casted during the years of Emperor Guang Qi in the Southern and Northern Dynasties

(A. D. 420-550), and walked around the yard of a Temple for three rounds neither gasping nor sweating.

3. Key to the Exercise: the Shaolin Master says that the training method of this Arts is simple and easy. It is a specific exercise of embracing-strength and chest-power . When successful, one will obtain Gang Qi inside his body. He will have got the strength of more than 700 catties when his arms embrace a tree. Unexpectedly in case of his coming across an enemy, he can embrace his enemy to death. The boxer says: "Practise a skill at leisure. One can defend himself while coming across an enemy accidentally. That means if one has mastered the consummate skill he can be all-conquering". If you don't believe in this, try to practise the skill for hundreds of days. It is better for you to embrace a small elm tree or a jujube tree. You will gain a wonderful result.

Eagle-Wings Arts

Bury two wood poles in the ground with a distance of over two feet between them and horizontally set a pole on their upper ends. Fasten two ropes to the horizontal pole and separately tie two bags of sand to the rope ends. The sand bags are to be 3 feet above the ground. The distance between two bags is to be about 2 feet. The structure just looks like a swing. The length of the ropes and the distance between the bags also depends on the trainee's height and weight. In a word the bag must be slightly lower than his shoulders when he is in the riding-horse stance. The distance between the bag and the shoulder must be about 7-8 inches. At the start each bag is about 10 catties in weight. The trainee stands between the bags in the riding-horse stance. Then he bends his elbows with two bags to the level of his shoulders and puts his fists on the upper part of his breast. He must try his best to let the bags press closely on his arms without the help of the drawing force of the ropes and try to raise them up. After getting exhausted, just take a rest and practise again. Every day, practise the skill in the morning and evening for more

53

than thirty times each time. Gradually increase the training times up to one hundred times a day. Within the first year he is to add 2 catties of sand to each bag every other month. A year later each bag will weigh up to about 34 catties. The strength of his arms will be very great. Now turn to practise the skill of "Owlet Force". That is to hang two sandbags, 20 catties in weight each as done before. As usual the trainee stands between the bags in the riding-horse stance. Put his bending elbows closely to the ribs and exert force to let the joints of his elbows touch the bottoms of the sand-bags to cast them away. The beginner can only cast the bags away for about 1 or 2 inches. Afterwards he will gradually be good at this Arts. After he is able to cast them away for about 2 feet as soon as the bags perch on his joints, he may begin to add 5 catties of sand to the bags each time . Satisfactory effects will result when each bag weighs fifty catties (Fig. 14).

Brief Introduction

1. Eagle-Wings Arts is one of the hard and external-strong arts in the seventy-two consummate skills of internal and external Gongfu which the Shaolin Templs has inherited secretly. It belongs to that of Yang Gang character. This is a specific exercise of the elbow.

2. The Boxing Guide states that the position of the elbow is in the middle between the shoulder and the wrist, so the elbow plays an important role in forming the connection between the two. If one lacks the skill, he can not direct the Vital Energy to his hands and will be unable to use his hands at will. Hanging elbows down is the best posture. Because of this, the force of the waist and the back can be directed to the shoulders, to the elbows and to the hands. In the actual fighting, it is bet-

54

ter for one to exert force within his shortest reach of the opponent because the force is efficient for quick lunging. Be quick when one acts, otherwise he will be snapped by the opponent. One had better adopt the half-step stance so as not to raise up his elbow and thus he can prevent his armpit from being attacked. There are also methods of elbow-pressing, elbow-blocking, elbow-lunging, elbow-turning in the practical uses. There-

Fig. 14

fore elbows are often compared to the "Second Defence Line " of the body. The Boxing Proverb runs: "Hands are used for attacking distant enemies;Elbows for nearby ones", "Hands must be close to elbows,elbows to the ribs,and the elbow techniques defend one's heart. " "Rather be beaten ten times by hands than once by an elbow ", "Elbows can attack anybody nearby and the enemies will be hit heavily unless they are

55

far away ", and so on. All these show the importance of elbows in the Shaolin Wushu. A poem goes: "Heart and Elbows rely on each other and the elbows defend the heart; Suitable to attack one's opponents nearby and not the distant ones. Speedy changes are highly necessary. If one moves slowly, he will lose his advantage. In the middle part of the body elbows predominate the feet and defeat the opponent with the help of the feet".

3. Elbow Techniques in the Shaolin Wushu refer to the aspect that one can defend himself or attack the enemy with his elbow-tips, his postarms and forearms while bending his elbows. Elbow Techniques play a determining role in the Shaolin Wushu. From the mechanics point of view elbows are nearer than fists to the shoulders when one stretches out his hands. As the arm of force is short one can make the best use of the strength of his shoulder's muscles with his elbows. From the angles of attacking his opponent he can reach his enemy's chest, back, abdomen, ribs, head and four limbs with his elbows. The common saying goes: "One can attack anybody nearby with his elbows". "From the direction of attacking one can launch an attack from lower position to upper position with his elbows (called "snaping elbow") and (called "sinking elbow"); and from left to right (called "crossing elbow")and from right to left (called "covering elbow"); not only from front to back (called "tucking in elbow"), but from back to front (called "pushing elbow"). The way of attack from front to back is much more speedy and concealed than the fist techniques are. From the viewpoint of physiology elbow-bones are hard and sharp. They have great strength against heavy blows, (especially, after making practice of "Eagle-Wings Arts" and "Overlord-Elbow Arts"and other Shaolin Gongfu. Elbows can be pushed

56

closer to the body of one's opponent, compared with the hands and feet. Evidently elbows are speedy and powerful in the nearby combat and valued for their making easy defence and forceful attacking. The poem says: " Elbows lie in the middle of one's arms. Take an action at one's own discretion. Seize the chance in a successive fighting. How painful it will be when the opponents are being butted by the elbow-tip". Another statement goes: "Hands are put down. Elbows are hidden. Sudden action difficult to be defended by one's opponent. Stretching and bending over and over again. Taking actions against nearby opponents rather than distant ones".

4. Elbows are at the juncture of one's postarms and forearms. Elbow-joints are consisted of distant lateral extremity of humerus (postarm bones), ulna and proximal lateral extremity of radius (forearm bones), they can be bent and stretched. In the theory of Shaolin Wushu, when the Elbows Training is mentioned, Elbow-Drop must be talked about . With the Elbow-Drop one can prevent his ribs from being attacked or injured so as to bring all of the joints of his body into coordinative play. When speaking of the Elbow Training, Elbow-Drop is connected with one's actions of shoulder-sinking and shoulder-collapsing. In the practice of "Eagle-Wing Arts," and "Overlord-Elbow Arts" of Shaolin Wushu, the flexibility of one 's muscles and tendons around his elbow-joints as well as the pliability of his arm muscles will be strengthened. Consequently the internal movements of one's arm muscles will also be improved. So one's strength, from his shoulder to his elbow, then to his wrist, will be harmonious. In this way when one bursts out his strength or changes the directions of his strength, he can act at ease. The "Secret of Shaolin Wushu " states that "To acquire one's wrist force and elbow

strength is definitely necessary. "

5. Key to the Exercise : the Shaolin Master says that this is a specific Arts to practise the lifting strength of his elbows. The strength of elbows is more powerful than that of palms and fists. But it's better for one to fight with his nearby opponent, not the distant one. After having achieved this Arts, one will be able to throw away anything heavy when it touches him. The skill is not inferior to "Paper-Covering Arts". Comparing with the other Arts, Eagle-Wings Arts is preferable. The lungs will be better-developed due to one's elbows bending practice.

Overlord-Elbow Arts

At the beginning lie on your back on the ground. Bend your forearms with the faces of fists upward and straighten your legs to let the feet-metatarsus closely touch the ground. Then direct the energy to your elbows to sustain your body in midair. Only your elbows and metatarsus are let to rest on the ground for about a quarter of an hour. After that, have a break. While your body is in midair, you have to breathe regularly, otherwise you are unable to keep concentrating your energy in this way long because your Qi cannot be gathered together. Every morning and evening practise this skill for tens of times each time. At leisure you may press your elbows against hard things as a supplementary training (Fig. 15-1). The second step is to use one elbow and one metatarsus to support your body. Support your body with your right elbow and your right metatarsus and than turn your body slowly to the right side without the aid of your left hand. You may resume to the normal position while you get tired. Then practise the skill in the same way on the left side. By turns practise the skill now on the left and now on the right each time for

Fig. 15-1

more than tens of times. That is a practice on an earth ground. A year later practise the Arts on a flat and smooth stone instead. Several years later do the same but on a rough stone. Finally dig a trough 3 feet in width and 6 feet in length and get the large and small smooth cobble stones mixed with mud and sand to fill the trough and put water in it to let it form a cobble-board. Then practise the skill on it. At start you may get painful. You can wash the wound with liquid medicine. Keep on making practice until you feel good at ease. Then get the crushed stones mixed with mud and sand to fill the trough as the above-said and make every effort to practise the skill till your elbows and heels are as hard as a stone. One should at least spend three years to achieve this Arts (Fig. 15-2).

Brief Introduction

1. Overlord-Elbow is one of the hard and external-strong arts in the seventy-two consummate skills of internal and external Gongfu which the Shaolin Temple has inherited secretly. It belongs to that of Yang Gang character. This is a specific exercise of one's elbows.

60

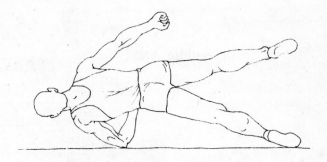

Fig. 15-2

2. Key to the Exercise : the Shaolin Master says that though the skill is one of the techniques of the Elbows Training, its key point is quite different from that of Eagle Wing Arts, which only stresses the exercise of one's elbow-sides and elbow-lifting force. Overlord Elbow Arts only places emphasis on using the strength of elbow-tips downward and backward. Don't confuse them.

Saddle Arts

First thrust your fist to the side of a light U-shaped stone or kick it with the instep of your foot. Though the stone is half buried in the earth, it can be removed after your long-run exercise. Satisfactory effect will come if your fist thrusted to the stone can remove it out of the earth. Then get a heavier U-shaped stone for making the same practice. After having succeeded in removing it in the same way, you can choose a much heavier U-shaped stone, about 200-300 catties in weight and continue to practise the same skill every day. After years' training you will achieve this Arts (Fig. 16).

Brief Introduction

1. Saddle Arts is one of the hard and external-strong arts in the seventy-two consummate skills of internal and external Gongfu which the Shaolin Temple has inherited secretly. It belongs to that of Yang Gang character. This is a specific exercise of one's fists.

2. The Boxing Guide states that fists are those of bending fingers,

Fig. 16

clenching themselves tightly, gathering the energy and attacking upon one's enemy. While a fist is clenched, the finger-tips must gather in the middle of the palm and the thumb should be bent to make its tip touch the second joint of the middle finger. In the way one's fingers will not be separated each other in fighting. There are several other kinds of methods to clench fists for their different uses. The Wushu Proverb runs: "Fists are like meteors and eyes like lightening," "Fist thrusting originates from one's mind and the force comes out of one's palms," Fist thrusting requires you to find the target. Missing the target means lacking of ability".

63

"No strength, no fist." "No use to have only hardness without softness". All these indicate that one's fists play an important role in the Shaolin Wushu. The poem states that "Thrusting out fist by raising one's shoulder and closing one's elbow at the same time. They help each other speedily and smoothly in a natural course like the flowing of the water. Attacking the opponent's head with one's straight fist at a blow. Not to give an average blow with one's fist. "

3. In the Shaolin Wushu "Power" is intently to be put into use. It especially refers to one's explosive force which is produced by the fast action and reaction of his muscles after making practice. The practical use of "Power" in Fist Technique, i. e. Holding Hammer (a code for Fist) in Shaolin Wushu, requires that before attacking the five fingers be slightly curved and the fist be loosely clenched, so as not to make elbows and shoulders become stiff. In the case of attacking the "Twisting Waist, Extending Shoulders and Swirling Arms" can make the energy "produced from his" waist, transmitted to his shoulders, hastened to his elbows and arrived at his hands". At the moment of attacking an opponent, start at once to clench his fists tightly with his whole energy and concentrate it on the surface of his fists and then give the opponent a sudden attack, thus injuring the opponent's bones and internal organs. There are ex- plainations about the practical use of Fist Force in the Wushu Guide : "Never let the fists get a little away from the target. As soon as the opponent's body is beaten by one's fists, he will be injured seriously. But the fists require the attacker to be as dexterous as possible" . In the "Shaolin Arhat External Eight-Fists Arts" there are techniques of "Beat- ing on the face by one's extending steps, on the abdomen by one's twist- ing steps, on the ribs by one's grasping energy, on the groin by one's arc-

64

ing scrotum, on the ears by one's Meteor Fists, on the waist by one's overturning his body, on the heart by one's Separating-Hammers, on the stomach by one's Lifting Lan-Hammer. "All these skills are practical uses of Power in the Shaolin Wushu.

4. Hands shift to Fists by clenching. "Fists are meant the clenching of one's fingers and thumb tightly with one's Qi concentrated in a circle". The technique of clenching fist requires to straighten one's four fingers first and gather them together except his thumb and then twist them and make the second phalanx of his middle finger and finally clench all of them tightly. There is also the so-called "Wa-lin" Fist in the Shaolin Wushu. It has many advantages for one to prevent his thumb from being broken and to deal with the Hanging-Technique and Carrying-Technique easily. Besides, there are the other Fist-Forms including Single Phoenix-Eyes Fists-Form, Double Phoenix-Eye Fist-Form, Phoenix-Pecking Fist-Form, Eagle-Claw Fist-Form and Spiral Fist-Form. There are the other kinds of Fist -Forms according to their positions, for instance, Fu-Fist (Palms downward); Yan-Fist (Palms upward); Standing-Fist (Fist-Eyes upward); Counter-Standing Fists (Fist-Eyes downward); Upper Thrusting-Fists (the surface of one's fists downward); Counter-Arm Yan-Fists (Palms upward but the surfaces of one s fists downward); Counter-Arm Fu-Fists (Palms downward but the surfaces of one's fists upward), etc. After making practice of Shaolin Fists Arts such as Saddle Technique, one's hands will have tremendous strength and the hardness of his bones and the force of his hand will be improved. One can get rid of sickness and prevent his hands from being hurt. One will be so skillful after the long-term exercise that he will be able to astonish all while thrusting out his fist. When one makes practice, he is required to make his elbows and

shoulders loose in the movement, otherwise his hands will be stiff and slow and he can not attain the desirable result.

5. Key to the Exercise: the Shaolin Master says that the exercise of this skill is similar to that of the Gang Rou Technique, but different in result. After the practice of Saddle-Exercise Arts one's fist is as hard as a hammer. The trainee, who has practised this Arts, will show the characteristic of flat bones on the face of his fists. After accomplishment one should avoid hitting others carelessly. Don't act as you please.

Pellet-Fist Arts

The training method of this Arts is very simple. It is similar to that of the Saddle Arts. The latter lays special stress on the exercise of one's fists strength only. The former lays particular emphasis on the exercise of one's finger-joints. The trainee has to half clench his fists with the first joints of his fingers twisted to reach their last joints. Simultaneously he keeps his palms straight with his thumbs twisted to his palm, like what is to be done in the Seizing-Hand Arts in the Seizing-Technique. One can beat a flat and smooth wood board with his projecting finger-joints. At the beginning one had better beat the flat board. When he beats the board, he is required to bend his elbows first and then thrust his fists immediately. Not necessary to stretch his arms as done in the Saddle Arts. As the finger-joints are covered with thin-layer muscles they may be easily injured when coming into contact with the hard wood board. Therefore in the first few months the beginner should be alert as to avoid hardness against hardness. Step by step one can practise the skill on a hard wood board, then on a rough stone and at last on an iron-slab. Don't

67

make haste. If one can beat an iron-plate to be concave with his finger-joints, he is said to have achieved this Arts(Fig. 17).

Fig. 17

Brief Introduction

1. Pellet-Fist Arts is one of the hard and external-strong arts in the seventy-two consummate skills of internal and external Gongfu which the Shaolin Temple has inherited secretly. It belongs to that of Yang Gang character. This is a specific exercise of one's fists.

2. The Fist -Form of "Pellet-Fist Arts called " Tiger Claw Fists "in

68

the Shaolin Fist-Techniques, is one of the skills of Removing-Bone secretly handed down from the Shaolin Temple. "Removing-Bone Illustration "relorded that" The essentials are those of pinching, removing, pushing and rubbing," " Removing-Technique requires to use one's joints between the Palm and Fingers (Tiger-Claw Fist and Cock-Heart Fist) to beat the other's bone-joints and make the latter's joint bones dislocated. The Pellet-Fist Arts is one of Basic Exercises of Removing Bones in the Shaolin Wushu. The poem goes that "How wonderful the skills of Pushing, Rubbing, Pinching and Removing are. One's bones will fall to the ground after their being kneaded and removed. If one gains advantage from this Arts, he can seize or catch his opponent at his will after has mastered it skillfully. If an opponent comes from the left, he follows to the left. He will incline to his side while coming across his opponent from the right. With the help of Removing Bones Arts, he can immediately give his opponent a deadly blow. It's preferable to use the skill correctly. Then he can succeed in both polite letters and martial arts. "

3. Pellet-Fist is one of the difficult arts for trainees to achieve. As far back as from the reigns of Tang, Song and Ming Dynasties downward there were successful Buddhist Monks, like Tan Zhone, Fu Guan, Yue Kong, Yue Lin, and so on in the Shaolin Temple". "Diary of a Qing Official" recorded that "Shi (Shi Dakai), the elder master of Shaolin School, counter attacked Ban Shen (Shi Dakai's disciple). Ben Shen knew that he was no match for Shi. He quickly dodged Shi's fists. Shi thrusted his fist on a stone tablet which was broken into pieces at once". So the poem says, "Clench tightly a pair of fists and try to hack the Western Mount; Strike a wood board with his fists at the start. And in return your fists become as hard as iron at last; Against a brick, strike it with Sleep-

ing-Fist. Against a wall, strike it with Butting-Fist. Hacking-Fist relies on its Qi and strength to break a stone into four petals. Keep on practising this Arts for thirty years, Marvellous result will be achieved. "

4. Key to the Exercise : the Shaolin Master says that this is a specific exercise of the second joints of one's fingers and it's one of the dreadful skills too. It is better for a learner to practise this Arts with his left hand, and efficient for him to strike an opponent's bone-joints. It is called "Tiger-Claw Fist Arts" in the Fist Technique and detailed in the Removing-Stone Technique.

Gang-Rou Arts

First bundle the waste-paper tightly with strings. Make it shaped like a brick about 2 feet in width and a little longer in length. Then tie a long string in the middle, which is used for pulling. This thing is called Paper-Clump. Then set the Paper-Clump on a table, its length being about 6. 6 metres and its width about 3 feet. The two boards at each end of the table are fixed to the stands and there are more than ten movable boards between the two. At first one stands at one end of the table in riding-horse stance, pulls the Paper Clump with the long string with his left hand and thrusts the Paper-Clump with his right fist. When the Paper-Clump is being struck, it may leap away farther. Now he pulls it back with the string in the left hand. Continue to strike it till he is completely exhausted. He can practise the skill with his left and right hands by turns. Do like this once every morning and evening. At the beginning the Paper-Clump is made of the waste-paper of not more than 20 catties in weight, so that it's easy for one to strike it. Thereafter put a piece of lead inside the Paper-Clump to increase its weight gradually from tens of cat-

71

ties to one hundred catties. It seems not difficult to keep on practising because he increases the weight step by step. At the time when a trainee can
hit the Paper-Clump to a greater distance and pull it back at his will, he
is considered to have half achieved the Arts only. Although with the
strength of his fists and arms he can astonish others, yet he has not
reached the peak of this Arts. Now take the narrowest board in the middle of the table away and a gap appears on the surface of the table in the
middle. Continue to strike the Paper-Clump as done before. Try not to let
the Paper-Clump fall into the gap. After a few months one can strike the
Paper-Clump to cross the gap. Then take another movable board away
till all the movable boards are taken away. There will appear a wide gap
about ten-odd feet in the middle of the long table. Satisfactory effect will
result when one can strike the Paper-Clump to leap across the gap and
then draw it back at his will without letting the Paper -Clump fall down
into the gap (Fig. 18).

Brief Introduction

　　1. Gang-Rou Arts is one of the hard and external-strong arts in the
seventy-two consummate skills of internal and external Gongfu which
the Shaolin Temple has inherited secretly. It belongs to both Yang Gang
character and Yin Rou Qi as well. This is a specific exercise of one's
fists.

　　2. During the time when you practise the Gang-Rou Arts, you can
combine it with the Thousand-Layer Paper Arts at the same time so as to
achieve a better effect in this Arts. The quality of paper is soft in spite of
its thickness and the Thousand-Layer Paper Clump can be used indoors
and outdoors, so it's especially suitable for a beginner. It is very simple to

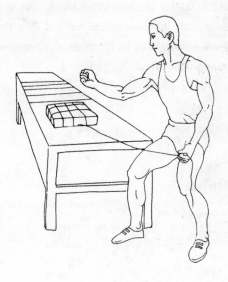

Fig. 18

make a Thousand-Layer Paper Clump. Get several dozen pieces of old newspaper, fold and bind them together to form a paper clump of 28 cm in length and 25 cm in width. Hang it on the wall for practising boxing. A beginner may use a thicker one, more than 5 cm in thickness. The key points are the same as those of the Gang-Rou Arts : One's steps must be steady, his fists should be clenched tightly and his wrists require to be straight. The power originates from his waist and then to his fists through his straightened shoulders. One is to use the striking force first lightly then heavily and make progress step by step.

　　3. Key to the Exercise : the Shaolin Master says that this Gongfu is

73

an exercise of one's fist. Though it seems as if it is a Hard Exercise, actually it combines the Hard with the Soft. While fighting, one can defeat his opponents easily with this Gongfu. This Gongfu belongs to that of Yang Gang character with the combination of Yin Rou Power and is marvellous for the co-ordination of its Hardness and Softness in harmony, so it is called Gang -Rou Arts.

Sand-Bag Arts

First, set a wood frame, on each side of the four sides of which a few sand-bags are hung. Each bag is about 5-6 catties in weight. The trainee has the option on the weight of each sand bag. The ropes must be pliable and strong. The bags are to be up to the height of his shoulders. Stand in the centre of the frame in riding-horse stance or in bow step. At the start thrust a sand-bag with his fist and make it swing out. While the bag swings back, exert force to strike it again. His wrist must be nimble. Then turn to practise with both fists instead. Strike the two bags in front of him simultaneously. After a few months strike the two bags by turns. First thrust out his right fist and while drawing his right fist back, thrust out his left fist. At the time when he draws back his left fist, the right sand-bag is swinging back and he strikes it with his right fist. Do it continuously for more than hundreds of times a day. After accomplishment of the skill of striking the two bags by turns one can shift to thrust his fists at the bags on both the right and left sides like the way mentioned above. Again, shift to thrust fists to the front first and then to both sides. First thrust one's fists to the front and then draw them back to hit both the right and left sides. Finally, shift to thrust his fists to the left and right and then to the front and the back. Practise to strike on four directions over and over again. Now he can strike the four bags one by one in four directions. It requires him to be quick in his movement, or he might be struck by the swinging bags. The above are the basis skill of this Arts . It is time now to go in for the advanced practice as follows. When one is versed in hitting the four bags, add 2 hanging bags behind him. Thrust his fists to the former 4 as done before, then strike the two bags at his back with his elbows. After that, add the third bag in the front centre and strike it with his head. Then add another two bags at either side of the left and right and strike them with his shoulders. Then add the last bag at the back of his head. Now one can take turns to strike 10 bags one by one. Satis factory effect will come when one can strike the bags in his free-steps instead of in his fixed-steps. That means that leaping and moving all round he can strike the bags with his feet, knees, shoulders, arms, etc. In that case he must be dexterous and quick in action as the Pear-Blossom Fist Arts requires him to do. Now one has achieved the final result(Fig. 19).

Brief Introduction

1. Sand-Bag Arts is one of the hard and external-strong arts in the seventy-two consummate skills of internal and external Gongfu which the Shaolin Temple has inherited secretly. It belongs to that of Yang Gang character. This is an exercise of the fists and other parts of one's body.

2. Sand-Bag Arts is one of the indispensable and specific skills in

76

Fig. 19

the Shaolin Wushu. And it also serves as one of the most important courses for learners. In order to make the sand-bags we should get to know its structure. The bag can be shaped like a ball, a square, or a pear in the Wushu Sport. The cylinder-shaped sand bag is the best, about 80-100 cm in length and 50-60 cm in diametre, the outside material of which is made of good quality cloth such as the canvas, the heavy woolen cloth, etc. And fill the sand inside, weighing about 20-35kg. One can also

77

mix sawdust with the sand.

3. After having finished the Sand-Bag Arts a trainee's power in his shoulders, elbows, wrists, fists, knees and feet will evidently be improved and strengthened and the harmony of his hands, eyes, body and legs will also be developed. Each of them plays an evident role in the position of exerting force and attacking strength. At the same time this Arts serves as a training method for a learner to foster the spirit of bearing hardships and indomitable will.

4. Notes : (1)The training place should be quiet. (2)Get the sense of actual fighting when training. (3)Do the warming-up exercise before training. (4)Pay attention to the correctness in action. (5)Handle well the regularity of the movement of sand-bags while training. (6)One's hands, eyes, body and steps should be in good harmony. (7)One should make practice step by step according to his own strength.

5. Key to the Exercise: the Shaolin Master says that the skill, just like the Gang-Rou Arts, is not easy for a trainee to achieve if he has only Yang Gang character. One must be in the condition of co-ordinating Hardness and Softness in harmony. After having achieved this Arts, one should take himself to be in the situation of facing the sand-bags on all sides while encountering his opponents. Sand-Bag Arts is really a common skill in the Shaolin Gongfu for its practical use.

TWENTIETH

Sunlight-Hands Arts

The training process presents no difficulty. Light an oil-lamp (or a candle). The flame is about half an inch long. Set the oil-lamp at the end of a table. Stand about 3 feet away from it in riding-horse stance. Flow your Qi to Dantian. Concentrating on yourself. Thrust out your fist towards the lamp and make practice in this way repeatly for about half an hour. Practise the skill continuously every morning and evening. If you can thrust out your fists and put out the flame, you will have reaped the first fruit. Then move yourself back about eight paces and practise in the same way . Now if you can thrust your fists and put out the flame, you are said to be successful. If you make a attack, your opponent can be hit to the ground though he is not touched by your fists. This is really called Yin Hands (Fig. 20).

Brief Introduction

1. Sunlight-Hands Arts is one of the hard and external-strong arts in the seventy-two consummate skills of internal and external Gongfu

79

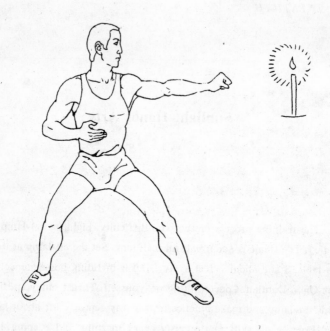

Fig. 20

which the Shaolin Temple has inherited secretly. It belongs to that of Yin Rou character. This is a specific exercise of one's fists.

    2. Key to the Exercise; the Shaolin Master says that though the skill of this Arts is not as violent as that of the Single-Finger Hand Stand Arts and Cinnabar Palm Arts but it's not inferior to them. It is thus called "Striking a Cow from the Other Side of the Hill"

Yin-Fist Arts

While training one stands before a well in riding-horse stance and strongly thrusts out his fists towards the surface of the water inside the well a hundred of times in the early morning or after midnight . At the start one may achieve nothing, but after having practised it for one or two years, his fist's thrusting will cause the water astir. Afterwards the water will become agitated and noisy. Gradually the water in it will sound like waves. Finally, practise this exercise for years, the water in it will surge like the rolling of waves (Fig. 21).

Brief Introduction

1. Yin-Fist Arts is one of the soft and internal-strong arts in the seventy-two consummate skills of internal and external Gongfu which the Shaolin Temple has inherited secretly. It belongs to that of Yin Rou Energy. This is a specific exercise of the fists. It is said that the late Master Hai Deng, a well known Shaolin Boxer, was versed in this skill when he was young.

81

Fig. 21

2. Key to the Exercise : the Shaolin Master says that this is an exercise of the fists and is commonly called "Yin Hand". It will take more than ten years to master this Arts. Apart from facing the well, one can practise this Arts towards the Sun in the morning, towards the Moon at night. One will master the Yin-Rou Energy if he practises this Arts for years.

Iron-Sand Palms Arts

Fill a cloth-bag with iron sand. Place it on a hard bench. Beat it with a single palm or two palms every morning and evening lightly and then heavily, slowly and then quickly. Whether one practises it with single or double palms depends on one's own choice. A hundred days later, one may get an initial result. After one year he will surely be successful, but he must not misuse this Arts(Fig. 22).

Brief Introduction

1. Iron-Sand Palms Arts is one of the hard and external-strong arts in the seventy-two consummate skills of internal and external Gongfu which the Shaolin Temple has inherited secretly. It belongs to that of Yang Gang character. This is a specific exercise of the palms.

2. The Boxing Guide states that with respect to this Arts, the two schools, i. e. North School and Shaolin Temple School had their own ways of training respectively. The North School which had a good command of the Arts was in favour of closing four fingers tightly in a row

with the thumb bent to attach to the palm's edge. While the Shaolin School, headed first by master Ban Hui, held to bend the four fingers to look like the Eagle's Claw. The former was called the Willow Leaf Palm. The latter was called the Tiger Claw Palm. In short, although they are different in name, the use of Energy is just the same. The same is that their fingers are stretched out and

Fig. 22

their force is concentrated in the hollow of the Palm. The Boxing Proverb runs: "Qi concentrates on the hollow of the palm. Energy arrives at limbs", "Fists originate from heart. Energy originates from palms", "Legs count seventy percent and hands thirty percent in a single combat. The palms make a fine display of the whole scene", etc. These simply indicate that the palms play an important role and show well their function in the Shaolin Wushu. So the poem says: "Hands move according to the command of the wrists. The toughness of one's palms with sharp bones gives rise to Wrist Energy. Movement must be quick and nimble. Beat with high efficiency. Conceal Hardness and Softness in Conformity. You are bound to win the combat. Stiff wrists and non-competent energy will mean a futile effect. "

3. In the Shaolin Boxing, no matter whether in the case of drawing back or stretching one's palms one should make himself relax consciously. While attacking one is to stretch out his palms suddenly and let his energy arrive at the hollows of the palms. Then the palms will become really powerful. Shaolin Wushu Guide states that the palm technique is the art of using fingers to jab(point)at the throat of one's opponent first and then pressing his whole palm downward and while his palm arrives at the opponent's chest he is to exert all his strength. At the instant of exerting all his strength he is to shout at the top of his voice so as to astonish the opponent. Thus his palm's energy is said to have come into full play. But only the veteran can do it. Be careful not to misuse the Arts. Don't treat a human life to be not worth a straw. "The relaxing of all joints before attacking is beneficial to make the joints nimble and changable for discharging stronger energy against his enemy with his palm. The soft energy hidden well in the hardness is in harmony. A poem states: " Qi is thrown out from Dantian. Energy leads to Palms. Discharge force to one's palms. Shout while releasing Qi. Push palms upward so forcefully that the opponent might fall down readily. Close to the opponent in riding-horse stance(Get close to the opponent and thrust powerful palms). Take care of oneself by standing in riding-horse stance). Do remember three words: Closing, Pressing, Throwing Up, all of which

make use of the small Heaven-Stars (Small Heaven Stars refer to one's sharp bones of cubit pulse).

4. The palms require the thumbs to be straight and the other four fingers slightly bent like hooks, but not completely alike. The form of the Long-Fist Palm requires the four fingers to be stretched tightly together and the thumb to be slightly bent to attach to the index finger. It is called Claw-Palm in the Shaolin Wushu. Its advantage is that its hand-form can be changed quickly and be easier to make a catch. Another palm-form requires one's four fingers to be closed together with his thumb bent to the "Tiger-Mouth". The palm faces inside with the hand appearing like the back of a tortoise. It is called Tortoise's Palm. In addition to this, there are Willow-Leaf Palm, Eight-Figured Palm, Wa Lin Palm, Snake-Like Palm and Dragon Claw Palm, etc. The changeable palm-positions are as follows: Bending Palm (the palm faces down), Raising Palm (the palm faces up) Standing Palm (the palm-fingers face up, the wrist-joint bends towards the back of palm, the palm and forearm become a right angle); Standing Straight Palm (the thumb faces up); Counter Standing Palm (the thumb faces down), Vertical Palm (the palm fingers face down, the wrist-joint does not bend); Horizontal Palm (the thumb faces down, set on the head, the hollow of the palm faces up). The name of the Shaolin Temple Iron-Sand Palm Arts implies the using of the iron-sand to make practice in order to make one's palm to be as solid as iron-. One can seriously injure his opponents with his palms. A veteran of this Arts can break a brick and crush a stone with his palm. Through the practice of Iron-Sand Palm Arts, the palm 's skin will become thicker and thicker with the skin tissues highly adaptable to outside environment. The wrist and finger-joints will be more flexible. The muscle will

86

be stronger than ever. All the above will bring forth the improvement of the manipulation of Energy in the Wushu Boxing. In the practice of Iron-Sand Palm Arts the ground green-beans mixed with Chinese pricklyash can be used to take the place of sand. Practise this Arts every day. Never stop practising. One will get evident results after hundreds of days. After one or two years one will achieve this Arts. When success-ful, one should also keep on practising this Arts.

5. Key to the Exercise : the Shaolin Master says that one should con-centrate on directing his Energy with the help of his internal-strong Qi while training. The so-called Arts of Steel-Iron Palm, Iron-Hand Flying-Sand and Black-Tiger-Hand is actually the Iron-Sand Palm Arts.

Bamboo-Leaf Hands Arts

Fill a coarse cloth with iron sand mixed with sharp iron pieces. The weight of the bag well hung on a hard wood stand is about 30 catties and the size of it is 2 square feet. The height of the stand is a little more than 6. 6 metres and the sand bag has to be hung in its middle with a large rope. The learner stands by the side of the stand in riding-horse stance and strikes at the bag with his fist. The hardness of sharp iron pieces and coarse iron sand often hurts his hands. The bag, at the start, only slightly swings after being struck. Later on it will sway to and fro to the extent of several metres. When the bag swings back, he is to block it with his palm, not letting it swing out of the stand. As soon as the bag touches his palm, he may exert force to rub it forward or hit it backward so as to let it rotate continuously before him. When it stops rotating, pat it, beat it or rub it as before. Practise it until he does not feel painful. Then increase the weight of the iron bag by about 20 catties. After a few months, add 20 catties of iron sand again. When the weight of the bag is increased up to 120 catties, if one can pat or beat it

88

with his palm at ease, he will have achieved the skill. It takes three or four years for one to practise this Arts from beginning to end(Fig. 23).

Fig. 23

Brief Introduction

1. Bamboo-Leaf Hands Arts, also called Copper-Sand Palm, is one of the hard and external-strong arts in the seventy-two consummate skills of internal and external Gongfu which the Shaolin Temple has inherited secretly. It belongs to that of Yang Gang character. This is a spe-

cific exercise of the palms. It is said that Shaolin Master Gu Ruzhan, who was good at it, was appointed as General Coach in the Wushu Institute, Hunan Province. He was able to break several bricks and big vats with his palms.

2. Key to the Exercise: the Shaolin Master says that it is a specific exercise of the palm, the same as the Saddle Exercise and Touching Stone Exercise. When successful, one should avoid using his right hand to take anything, for his palm will destroy things or hurt others. So it is advisable to practise it with only the left hand.

Pushing-Mount Palms Arts

Get a wood stand in the form of a rectangle table. Bury their four feet in the ground. Make it unshakable. Wrap its both upper horizontal beams with galvanized iron. At first place a piece of square green stone flat on one side of the stand. The weight of the stone is about 80 catties. Stand in front of the stone in bow step, one and a half feet away from it. Then put two palms or a single palm by turns flat on the surface of the stone and make pushing. While making pushing the learner should exert his force from his arms, wrist and palms. Don't incline the upper part of his body. Don't press his body onto the stone. Don't be eager for instant success. If he is unable to move the stone, he must try his best again and again to make it move. After practice he will get a successful result. When he can push the stone quite afar, say, several feet or tens of feet away with his elbows bent on the surface of the stone, he may then add on it another stone of about 20 or 30 catties. If he can push the stone to a long distance at ease, he can increase the weight of the stone up to 300 catties. Now he has achieved the skills in the first stage. And his arms are mightier. But it is impractical for him to use this Arts in combat. This is a basic skill only just like the foundation of a house . The further step is to learn the Sudden Energy. To practise this Sudden Energy, one must rely upon the rear of his palm and his wrist. The training method is similar to the above. Now remove away all the added stones with the remaining of only the original one on the stand. Now, one presses all his fingers upon the surface of the stone and with the hind part of his palms. He touches the stone in bow step and then directs the energy between his forearms and wrists to push it with his full arms' force. While exerting his force to make pushing he must heavily press the stone with his fingers and raise both hind palms 3 inches above the stand. Thus, the 80 catties stone will follow his hands flying afar to a dis tance of tens of feet. Should all the removed stones be added again and thus the block of stones of 300 catties can still be pushed away in the above way by him, he is considered to have achieved this Arts (Fig. 24).

Brief Introduction

1. Push-Mount Palm Arts is one of the external-strong Arts in the seventy-two consummate skills of internal and external Gongfu which the Shaolin Temple has inherited secretly. It belongs to that of Yang Gang character. This is a specific exercise of the palms.

2. Key to the Exercise : the Shaolin Master says that this Arts is a specific exercise of both palms and wrists like the Gang-Rou Technique. After achievement one may just use a single palm to push his opponent far away while combating. This skill still can help one to make use of the opponent's energy to throw the opponent away without being injured. It is not an Arts for hurting or killing others. The veteran can push a pile

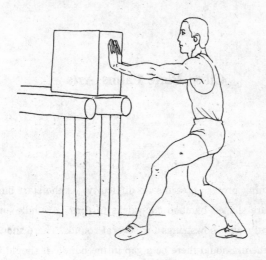

Fig. 24

of a over ten big stones far away if he touches the original stone on the table only, which will stand still and won't move at all, because he has the skill of both exerting energy and reserving Energy.

Close-Plate Palms Arts

The training process presents no difficulty. At the start bind thirty pieces of square-shaped bamboo chopsticks to form a bundle and tie its both ends tightly with bowstrings for several rounds. There should be no gap between them. Should there be a gap in the bundle it should be tightly staffed with extra chopsticks, Thus, the chopsticks in the bundle should be perfectly unmovable. Then one holds the two ends with his both hands and winds them oppositely. If his right hand winds one end inward, his left hand should wind the other end outward. In the course of winding one's force should be applied. Take a rest if one gets tired. Then close his palms forcefully to press the chopsticks from both sides and make every endeavour to rub them several times a day. At first one may not be able to make the chopsticks move at all, for they are bound very tightly. In fact it is very effective for one to practise this Arts for one or two years. In the case of winding one can make them twist slantwise. In the case of rubbing, one can also make them move. The next stage is to use the iron chopsticks instead of the bamboo chopsticks. One or two years

94

later again even the thumb-size iron chopsticks can be reduced into the size of small fingers with their length doubled. Thousands-of-days' training one certainly can reach the zenith(Fig. 25).

Brief Introduction

1. Close-Plate Palms Arts is one of the hard and external-strong arts in the seventy-two consummate skills of internal and external Gongfu which the Shaolin Temple has inherited secretly. It belongs to that of Yang Gang character. This is a specific exercise of the palm.

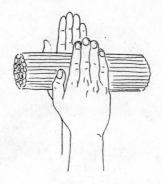

2. Key to the Exercise: the Shaolin Master says that it is also called Golden-Dragon Hand Arts, similar to the Arts

Fig. 25

of Palm Skill of Rubbing and Chopping Hand. The latter lays emphasis on Attacking and Defending Skill while the former lays stress on bringing somebody under control. After having accomplished this skill, one can crush the stone into pieces whenever he rubs it. Once I read the Diary of Jiang Jin-yuan, who was a chivalrous man on the South Yangtze River. With his hands he could rub a tree into pieces of firewood, split a bamboo into a broom and rub the finger-size iron-bar into an iron-string for making an iron door framework. It is thus clear that how powerful the Arts has been.

Mantis-Claw Arts

Pile up dozens of bricks, on the top of which are covered with mulberry bark paper about three inches in thickness. Near by the bricks stands the learner. His forearm is to be stretched out straightly with his upper arm tightly pressed on his ribs. Direct his energy to the wrist. Keep his hand about 3 inches away from the paper. While making practice, after directing his energy to his wrist he raises up his forearm with his thumb and all fingers tips facing upward and then immediately turns his wrist down to cut the mulberry paper on the brick with the edge of his palm. The left palm and the right palm do the above practice by turns. At the start do it twice every morning and cut the paper hundreds of times. He can increase the number of times according to his will. At first one may achieve nothing. After making practice for one year some of the bricks under the paper are broken into pieces when he cuts the paper with the edge of his palm. Keep on practising in this way until he is able to break all the bricks under the paper into pieces with the edge of his palm. Then, on each occasion of making the practice, add a 3-inch-thick mulberry bark paper bundle on the top of the brick pile and similarly take away about the same "thickness of bricks away until the thickness of the paper bundle is over 2 feet. It means that he is able to break all the bricks with the edge of his palm in spite of the fact that the thickness of the paper on the brick-pile is over 2 feet. The above is only the first step of success. This is an exercise of "Dead Energy ", Now he must turn to practise the "Life Energy ". It is really difficult for a learner to change from practising "Dead Energy" into practising "Life Energy". When a trainee makes practice, a tile is to stand vertically on the ground with two bricks on both sides to support it. Don't let it fall, then he cut it with the edge of his palms. At the start the tile may fall down and unbroken. Afterwards he will be able to cut any part of it as he likes. He must get to the stage that without the support of two bricks, the main part of the tile will remain intact and stand erect although a certain part of it has been cut off. Now one is said to have achieved seventy percent of this skill. - Then make practice of this Arts on a thin brick, step by step on a thicker brick. At last, on a stone. If one is able to cut the stone into pieces with the edge of his palms, he is considered to have won the goal(Fig. 26).

Brief Introduction

1. Manti-Claw Arts, also called Jin Gang Hands, is one of the hard and external-strong arts in the seventy-two consummate skills of internal and external Gongfu which the Shaolin Temple has inherited secretly. It belongs to both Yang Gang charact er and Yin Rou Energy. This is a specific exercise of the palms.

2. Key to the Exercise: the Shaolin Master says that it is an exercise of the palm-edge and wrist. It is like the Guan Yin Palm Arts, but differ-

Fig. 26

ent in applying force. Manti-Claw Arts is that of directing the energy to
the forearms from the upper part of the body flatly downward to the
palms. It is what is really called Gang Energy. The Arts is a shortest way
to de feat the opponent at the instant of the bending of the wrist. It is like
chopping with a Mantis-Axe , so it is named Mantis-Claw. In the Boxing
Technique it is also named Chopping Palms Arts and called Chopping
Hand Arts in the Shaolin Technique. It really presents Rou Energy with
hardness dwelled in softness. It takes one a long time to practise this
Arts. Therefore one should first use the mulberry bark paper to practise

99

the Rou Skill and master the Gang Arts through breaking the bricks under the paper. It is an exercise of Gang through the medium of Rou so
that the Softness and Hardness can co-ordinate naturally. This Arts was
originated from Shaolin, spread over the South Yangtze River, especially
in the place of Deng, Xi, Kun, Lin minority localities. The commonly
called "Thirteen Mantis-Claw "and "Mantis School" are only a display of
the fist skill and do not belong to the realm of Gongfu.

Guan-Yin Palms Arts

Place one's hand on the wood implement. Holding his palm in slanting position and continously chop the wood with his palm-edge. Shift to chop the stone after he can chop the wood to have a deep concave mark of his palm edge. After one or two years, practice when he chops the stone with his hand, some fragments of the stone will fly out, just as the stone is chiseled by a hammer. When he uses the edge of his palm to chop the stone which appears to have been chopped with a sharp knife without leaving any irregular marks on the cut part, he can be said to be successful. Then shift to fill a deep plate with iron filings to more than one foot in depth. Chop the iron filings with his palm as before. At the start when he chops the iron filings, they may be splitted. But as soon as his palm is taken away, the iron filings will gather together again. After a long time of practising when he chops the iron filings, they will not gather together again after his hand is taken away. At last when he chops the iron filings, they will fly to opposite directions leaving a vertical line. Moreover there will be no iron filings on the bottom of the plate. If the iron filings are to be chopped separately at the same time, they will be divided into several parts just like a cut bean-curd. He is then a top master of this Arts (Fig. 27).

Fig. 27

Brief Introduction

1. Guan-Yin Palm Arts, also called Chopping Monster Sword, is one of the soft and external-strong arts in the seventy-two consummate skills of internal and external Gongfu which the Shaolin Temple has inherited secretly. It belongs to that of Yin Rou character. This is a specific exercise of the palm. The poem runs : "Breaking a brick into parts with a sin-

gle hand is a integration of seventy-two skills. Chop the rice bag early in the morning ;Chop the wood bed late at night;Chop the dining table at noon ;Chop the wall after dinner. The skins and bones may be injured. - Bloody training for a year round. Take a leisurely walk for chopping. - Chop a wood figure direct and sideways. Make practice for hundreds of days. Chop apart the brick with a single hand. "

2. Keg to the Exercise:the Shaolin Master says that it is an exercise of the wrist-edge,the same as the Chopping Hands Arts. When successful,one's palm may. be used as a knife. The Arts is similar to the Saddle Exercise and the Cinnabar-Palm Arts.

Five-Poison Hands Arts

On the date of Qingming Festival, get 10kg. of mud earth from the bottom of the river, which is pale-yellow in colour. Dry it and fill it into a jar. Then, on the date of the Dragon Boat Festival, mix five-poisons with the mud earth and pound them into a mess of paste. Again add 5kg. iron-sand, 5kg. vinegar, 2. 5kg. Kao-liang wine, 1kg. bronze filings and make them well mixed. Now place this prepared earth on a hard wood bench and pat and strike it with your palm every morning and evening. - Never stop practising nor slacken a little to do it. One will achieve this Arts in three years (Fig. 28).

Brief Introduction

1. Five-Poisons Hands Arts, also called Yin Hands or Five-Thunder Palms, is one of the hard and external-strong arts in the seventy-two consummate skills of internal and external Gongfu which the Shaolin Temple. has inherited secretly. It belongs to that of Yang Gang character and Yin Rou Energy. This is a specific exercise of the palm.

104

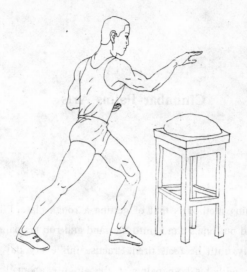

Fig. 28

2. Key to the Exercise: the Shaolin Master says that a great many people practise this skill from corners of the country, for it is very simple to practise it One should finish all necessary preparations before training. The learner had better practise this Arts with his left hand. Don't hurt others accidently.

Translator's Note :

  * Five-Poisons: It refers to Snake, Centipede, Lizard, Scorpion and Wasp. Here, it is just an emblem of five fingers.

Cinnabar-Palms Arts

The training method is that of getting a rough plate. Fill the fine-sand into it and put one's hands into the sand and rub his palms with the sand incessantly until he feels tired. Practise this every day persistently. If one rubs with his both palms in the air, i. e. about 1 foot away from the plate and the fine sand is seen to be moving under his palms, he is taken to have the first stage success. This is so called Spirit Concentration And Qi Gathering. If the opponent is slightly touched by this type of palms, the internal organs within his body will be seriously injured although there is no mark of injury in the external part of his body. The next stage is to use sand, then use the iron sand and even the iron ball. - Great achievements are made when the iron sand or the iron ball of 4-5 taels in weight each, will move out of the plate although his hands are not touching the plate (Fig. 29).

Brief Introduction

1. Cinnabar-Palm Arts, also called Plum Blossom Palm Arts and

Fig. 29

Red-Cinnabar Palm Arts, is one of the soft and internal-strong arts in the seventy-two consummate skills of internal Gongfu which the Shaolin Temple has inherited secretly. It belongs to that of Yin Rou character. This is a specific exercise of the palm.

2. Cinnabar-Palm Arts is one of the consummate arts of Yin Rou Energy. The Cinnabar -Palm Arts and Iron-Sand Palm Arts may be rated as one Yin, another Yang; one Gang, another Rou ; one brightness, another darkness; one outside, another inside. The main method of Cinnabar-Palm is that of directing inner Qi to one's Palms, to cause the opponent to suffer from serious internal-organ injury. At first a man

107

who is beaten by the Cinnabar Palm does not find the case serious, but a few days later the bright red palm-marks will appear on his body. The learner will be stronger and healthier for the Qi and Blood streaming within his body will improve the functions of his internal organs. A veteran of this Arts can let out Qi to generate "electricity" through his palms. "Wu Xia Painting Collection" in Qing Dynasty states that Shu Yin, who learned the Arts from a Buddhist Monk for twelve years, was taught this consummate skill "Cinnabar-Palm" secretly. Had he touched his opponents' body with his palms , he would have broken the opponent's bones into pieces.

3. Key to the Exercise: the Shaolin Master says that one has to spend fifteen years to learn this Arts. One also must not abuse it. It is quite different from the Black Cinnabar-Palm Arts, by which if an opponent is beaten, he can be helped by using medicines.

Single-Finger Jin Gang Arts

The training method is that the learner touches the walls and trees with his index finger lightly at first and then heavily every day. Three years later he will acquire the skill. If he touches something, there will be evident marks on it. On touching a piece of wood there must be a hole in it. On touching a stone it will be crushed. On touching a person's body. The person will die immediately. After training this single finger skill for three years, one will be crowned with success to the astonishment of all for his strong will to have a high attainment (Fig. 30).

Brief Introduction

1. Single-Finger Jin Gang Arts, is one of the hard and external-strong arts in the seventy-two consummate skills of internal and external Gongfu which the Shaolin Temple has inherited secretly. It belongs to that of Yang Gang character. This is a specific exercise of the fingers.

2. The Boxing Guide goes; the finger technique is different in name, for the name is given according to the number of fingers use-

Fig. 30

d. After all there are only two kinds of finger techniques, i. e. Inserting and Pointing. One can not make use of the Arts without the concentration of Qi and Energy. When making practice, it is necessary for one to exert energy to his finger-tips. The skill may not be hard and fast if one takes it easy. It is very helpful for one to learn the other Arts. The Boxing Proverb says, "Finger kills a point, Fist strikes a spot. " "Fists are weaker than Palms, Palms are not so fierce as Fingers", "Hair is the tip of Blood; Fingers are tips of Muscles". "Feet are like tiger-claws while

110

combating; Fingers are like steel-nails while fighting" etc. All these indicate that the fingers play an significant role in the Shaolin Wushu. So the poem runs, "Teeth are tips of bone. A bite with teeth with full energy may tear the muscles. Tongue is the tip of muscles, the tongue touches the upper-palate to connect Qi and energy; Hair is a tip of blood, hair stands straight to push off a hat. Fingers are tips of veins. When the energy of the fingers works, it will take the opponent's life away immediately. "

3. Finger Technique in the Shaolin Wushu requires the relaxation of fists and palms to reserve their softness to a certain extent. While combating one is to direct his energy to the tips of his fingers. Fingers Techniques in the Shaolin Wushu, include: Pointing, Jabbing, Crosscutting, Picking, Driving, Stretching, Shooting, Pressing, Catching, Hanging, Taking, etc. With the Finger Technique one usually attacks his opponent's weak or vital parts of the body with his fingers, such as the eyes, nose, ears, brain, throat, chest, abdomen, groin, etc. In the case of catching one is required to finish the three steps with his fingers: Spouting, Bucking and Draging. Take the example of grabbing the face: "Spouting" refers to strike the frontier sinus of one's nose with fingers; "Bucking" means to dig one's eyes; "Draging" indicates to catch hold of and draw back the opponent with one's finger-claws. So they are terrible skills actually. The poem runs: " To advance or retreat at speed. To stretch or withdraw nimbly and quickly. Blood stains and scars one's body. Wherever one's fingers touch bloodstained marks will appear".

"Fingers Arts" is always achieved through a comprehensive study of the other skills. The fingers Arts enrich the experiences of the other arts, such as, Arhat Arts, Nature Arts and Erh-Lan Arts. All of them include

111

the Arts of fingers' techniques. Those who take the fingers' techniques as major Arts are "Shaolin Thirteen-Claw" and "Eagle-Claws". About the use of finger's technique, "Secret Of Shaolin Boxing" states that "… A ganster kicked an old man again. The old man yielded. After having been kicked for three times, the old man slightly inclined to the ground and blocked the ganster slightly with his left hand and struck the instep of the ganster's foot with his two fingers. Then the ganster fell down moveless with his face turned pale and choked with pains. Later, someone helped him and carried him away. " "The Legend Of Liao-Zai" records that "… Li thought that Ni was timid, so Li wanted to fight with Ni. Ni stood up. At the moment Li kicked Ni with his leg and Ni cut Li's thigh with his five fingers. Li felt that his knees had been chopped by an axe and fell to the ground immediately. "

4. In the Shaolin Wushu a single finger is called Golden Needle Finger. Two Fingers, called Gold Cutter Fingers. Three Fingers, called Three Yang Fingers. Four Fingers-Stretching, called Golden Spade Fingers. Forefinger Joint-Striking, called Ghost-Head Fingers; the Middle Finger Joint-Striking, called Phoenix Nodding Finger. If finger-tips turns inward, it is called Kou Fist Fingers. If fingers are open, it is called "Claw", including Eagle-Claw, Tiger-Claw, Dragon-Claw and Crane-Claw, etc. In the Shaolin Wushu hands are tools for exerting force. Wrists are Blasting Fuses for directing Energy. Therefore, if one wants to have quick hands, he must have nimble wrists. Through the practice of Single-Finger Jin Gang Arts, not only can the flexibility of wrist joints and finger-joints be strengthened, but also their force and hardness can be improved. One will be able to apply strong grabing-force, fastening-force, picking-force and Left-Right Shaking force with his fingers. The

112

concentration of one's forces will produce a special Energy in the exercise of Wushu. It is said that Master Miao Xin of Shaolin Temple used his single finger Jin Gang Skill to write four words "Each Has Strong Points" on the surface of a smooth stone, which were carve-like and vigorous. Thus it can be seen that he had mastered the excellent skill of this Arts.

5. Key to the Exercise: the Shaolin Master says that the learner can break the opponent's internal organs with a single finger only. Please remember it! Unless one is driven beyond forbearance, his left index finger can not be used to hurt people. One must stick to making practice. This skill, in comparison with Yin-Hand Single Finger, is different in its application but is equally satisfactory in its result.

Immortal-Palms Arts

At first close one's four fingers tightly in a row and apply force every day to press them against hard things, such as tables, walls or benches. At the start it is not necessary to press his fingers against the fixed objects. After a long period of practising a certain point of a wood plank can be pressed to sink slightly. Practise step by step and the plank can be pressed to have a hole. Then practise the skill with a stone. Only when one can press a stone with his fingers to give rise to a deep concave curvature on its surface, he can be said to have accomplished this Arts. If one utilizes this Arts while fighting, he will give his opponent a good dusting (Fig. 31).

Brief Introduction

1. Immortal-Palm Arts is one of the hard and external-strong Arts in the seventy-two consummate skills of internal and external Gongfu which the Shaolin Temple has inherited secretly. It belongs to that of Yang Gang character. This is a specific exercise of one's palms.

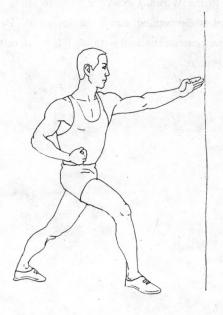

Fig. 31

2. Key to the Exercise; the Shaolin Master says that it is an exercise of the thrusting-force of finger-tips, similar to that of the soft Yin-Hand Single Stand Arts. The difference is that the former uses four fingers and the latter uses a single finger. To achieve the Arts is so easy and needs less time that many people like to practise it. After having mastered the Arts, one can be invincible, even the opponents who have practised the Iron-Cow Arts are no match for him. Iron-Cow Arts has Yang Gang

115

character only. Immortal-Palm Arts has both Yang Gang character and Yin Rou Energy. Its Softness can control the Hardness. Its Yin can defeat the Yang. In the Wushu Circles the proverb goes: "Iron-Cow Arts will be defeated while coming across the Immortal -Palm Arts". The trainee had better practise the skill with his left hand, or he might injure the others accidentally.

Touching-Stone Arts

It is easy to practise this Arts. Put one's middle and index fingers closely and straight. Bend one's ring finger and little finger closely to his palm and bend his thumb and press it on the ring finger, just like that of pointing something with one's two fingers. Then his middle and index fingers can be used to stab something hard. After a long-run exercise one will reap the first fruit. At the beginning get some earth and mix it with glue. Pound the mixture in a stone mortar and make them pliable and tough. Then shape it like a square. After having dried it, one may draw many circles on it with a pencil, mark them with numbers and then stab each circle in sequence. One may stab the first circle for several months and it will slightly sink down with a concave curvature. Then turn to stab the second circle. Although the times of stabbing and the number of days used may be decreased, the second circle will also sink down. Keep on practising in this way. Finally, as soon as a circle is stabbed, it will sink down immediately. But one must spend about two years in practising this Arts. Then a stone can be used for stabbing. Don't make haste. After

117

another two years of practising, if one stabs a stone, the spot of which where he stabs will also sink down with a concave curvature. Now he is said to have achieved this Arts(Fig. 32).

Fig. 32

Brief Introduction

1. Touching-Stone Arts is one of the hard and external-strong Arts

118

in the seventy-two consummate skills of internal and external Gongfu which the Shaolin Temple has inherited secretly. It belongs to that of Yang Gang character. This is a specific exercise of one's fingers. The skill is vigorous and has explosive force. One can improve the wrist-force and stretching-force of his fingers.

2. Key to the Exercise: the Shaolin Master says that the skill, which is similar to Picking Up Flower Arts and the soft Gongfu "Single-Finger Hand Stand Arts", is a specific exercise of one's finger-stabbing ability. Picking-Up Flower Arts lays stress on the surface of one's fingers and this Arts on the finger-tips. The difference is that Single-Finger Hand Stand Arts can injure his opponent without touching his opponent's body. But the result is the same.

Pipa Arts

Press your thumb on the four finger-nails(Fig. 33 — 1). And exert your force to flick the four fingers off your thumb (Fig. 33-2). The

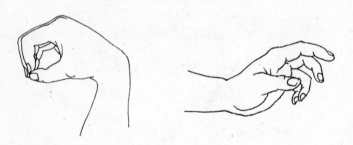

Fig. 33-1   Fig. 33-2

Arts is commonly called "Flicking Brain-Tablet". The process of practis-ing is as follows. Flick the forefinger, middle finger, the ring finger and little finger from the thumb in sequence. Alternately flick the little fin-

120

ger, ring finger, middle finger and forefinger from the thumb in sequence
again. It is better to flick the medicine bag with your fingers for one
hundred and eight times every morning and evening. After three years
you will achieve the Arts.

Brief Introduction

1. Pipa Arts, also called Three-Yin Fingers, is one of the hard and
external-strong Arts in the seventy-two consummate skills which the
Shaolin Temple has inherited secretly. It belongs to that of Yang Gang
character. It is a specific exercise of one's fingers.

2. Key to the Exercise; the Shaolin Master says that it is an exercise
of flicking one's finger nails of the first joints. After having accomplished
it, one will be strong enough to flick with his fingers and defeat an opponent, though this skill is inferior to that of the Single-Finger Hand
Stand Arts. But if one flicks the vital part of an opponent's body, one can
give his opponent a deadly blow. So be careful to use this skill. The
trainee always uses a single finger (the forefinger or the middle finger)
to practise the Finger-Flicking Arts. But the trainee has to use his four
fingers to practise Pipa Arts and flicks them out one by one in sequence
as if he is playing Pipa Arts. It is rather strenuous for a trainee to master
this Arts for the flicking force of his finger-nails is very weak. Therefore
if he wants to achieve the skill, he must stick to the practice and keep on
practising assiduously and diligently.

Pulling Up Nails Arts

Drive one hundred and eight three-inch nails into a thick jujube plank with a hammer. Try your best to pull them up one by one by using your thumb, your index finger and your middle finger until they are pulled up without difficulty. Now you have reaped the first fruit. Then again drive the nails into a wood plank with a hammer and sprinkle some water on them to make them rusty. After that, make great efforts to pull them up as before. You will achieve this Arts if you do not find it difficult to pull them up(Fig. 34).

Brief Introduction

1. Pulling-Up Nails Arts is one of the hard and external strong Arts in the seventy-two consummate skills of internal and external Gongfu which the Shaolin Temple has inherited secretly. It belongs to that of Yang Gang character. It is a specific exercise of one's fingers.

2. The "Secret Of Shaolin Boxing" runs: "Drive nails into a wood plank wall and try to pull them out every day. One can be said to have

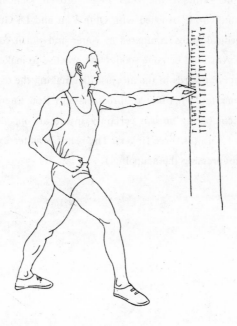

Fig. 34

acquired the skill if he can pull up the deepest driven nail. In the case of fighting with an opponent, he can break the opponent's skin by a slight touch with his fingers. The people along the West Yangtze River are fond of this Arts.

3. Key to the Exercise: the Shaolin Master says that it is one of the

exercise of one's hand. It lays stress on the grasping force of one's thumb and forefinger. The training process is very simple. But it is rather difficult to practise the skill. At the start one's broken skin may shed blood. But the wound can be washed with Qing Yan and Di Gu Pi (Chinese traditional medical herbs) simmered in water and sterilized. The inflammation of the skins will be gone soon. Now practise to make grasping with his three fingers upwards in the air, just like making the dragging of heavy things. He has to do his best to direct his Yin Rou Energy at the same time. While combating he can certainly injure an opponent if he grasps the opponent with his three fingers. The result is as terrible as that of seizing Xue Dao (pressing the acupoints).

Lifting-Up Thousand-Catties Arts

Chisel a rough stone into the form of a circular cone. The smallest one must be about ten catties in weight and the biggest one is about sixty or seventy catties. The bottom of it is about 7 — 8 inches in diameter. Thus, a cone-shaped stone is made. The trainee strives to pick its sharp end up with his thumb, his middle finger and his forefinger. When the stone is being picked, his fingers are all held downward. And the top of this cone-shaped stone must be kept a little distance away from the hollow of the palm. While picking it, try his best to pick it upward to leave the ground. At the start it is extremely difficult for him to pick up a cone-shaped stone weighing over 10 catties with his three fingers pressing on its pointed end and its smooth surface. He may not be able to pick and lift it up or even move it at all. He has to spend one and half a year in practising the Arts. When he can pick and lift it up, he must keep on practising this Arts for some time so as not to have a retrogression of his acquired skill. After that he must try to go around a place with the lifted stone. At the start the stone may slip out off his hand or he can only walk a few steps with the stone between his fingers. But after having achieved this Arts, he can pick and lift it up and go in a square for tens of steps, hundreds of steps and lastly tens of rounds. Then get a heavier stone to practise this Arts. Don't rush advance. Each time it is better to change a 3 catties heavier stone for practising, or he might be injured on account of a sudden increase of much weight. Step by step he will be able to pick and lift up 50—60 catties of stone and sustain it as long he likes, say, at least an hour. If he can pick and lift it up and then walk for two hours, he is considered to have made great success (Fig. 35).

Fig. 35

126

Brief Introduction

1. Lifting-UP Thousand-Catties Arts is one of the hard and external-strong Arts in the seventy-two consummate skills of internal and external Gongfu which the Shaolin Temple has inherited secretly. It belongs to that of Yang Gang character. It is a specific exercise of one's fingers and arms. It is also called Stone-Water-Chestnut Arts.

2. The "Diary of a Qing Official" says: "the Stone-Water-Chestnut is also called Stone Peach Arts". In the Li-An Temple of Hu-Pao, Hangzhou city, Zhejiang Province, "Five Stone Peaches" are seen in the yard. Most of them are about 5 — 6 catties and the heaviest one more than 20 catties. They are often picked and lifted up by the trainees with their 3 fingers. ". " ···a Buddhist Monk Shu declined to do so although Lin asked him again and again. Then a young Buddhist monk came out and was ordered to picked and lift up the smallest stone. He did it just like taking a steamed bread. This proved that the young monk was one with great strength. His fingers were as hard as iron. The story implied that the master of the young monk was able to lift a 20 catties stone-peach but he disliked to make a show himself before a visitor"

3. Key to the Exercise: the Shaolin Master says that it is an exercise of one's thumb, forefinger and middle finger, including the lifting force of one's arms. It is similar to Eagle-Claw Arts and Removing Mountain Arts. But this skill is to exert force on the three fingers and not on the finger-tips or the finger-sides. Many Wushu lovers in Southern China go in for this Arts.

Rubbing And Inserting Arts

At dawn get up and stand on a spacious ground, close your mouth, concentrate on yourself, close your palms together and rub them for twenty times. Then put the hollow of your right palm on your chest and the left palm on your back. The right and left palms are facing oppositely each other and they rub circlewise again and again for 40 — 50 times. Then exchange the positions of your left and right hands and practise in the same way. While rubbing your palms, don't open your mouth. Breath through your nose, direct energy to your chest. After a long-range exercise you may feel there is a ball of Qi deposited inside your chest. Now it is time to direct the Qi to your both arms and then to your fingers. Again, take a case filled with beans. Insert your palms into the beans by turns, i. e. one up and the other down and then one down and the other up. The number of times of inserting your palms depends on your strength. Do it until you are completely exhausted. It is necessary to remember the number of times so that you can count and gradually add the times of inserting. For example, for the first day, do it one hundred

128

times, and for the second day, do it one hundred and five times. You may get an initial result if you can do it for about one hour. Then take a case filled with rice. Practise the Arts in the same way. If you can insert your palms into the rice as before for about one hour, you have come to a head (Fig. 36).

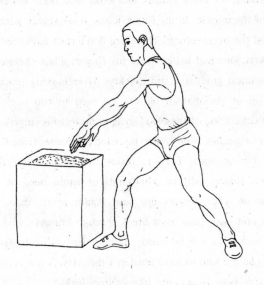

Fig. 36

Brief Introduction

1. Rubbing-Inserting Arts is one of the hard and external strong Arts in the seventy-two consummate skills of internal and external

Gongfu which the Shaolin Temple has inherited secretly. It belongs to that of Yang Gang character and is also a specific exercise of one's fingers.

2. The "secret Of Shaolin Wushu" says that those boxer masters in the countryside always teach the beginners to fill the wood bucket with sand and ask them to insert their palms into the bucket over and over again to make their fingers as hard as iron. Because of the sensitivity of the nerve ending of one's fingers and especially none existence of the flexibility of the muscles in the finger joints, one's finger-joints are liable to be injured for overexertion. Therefore don't rush advance while practising the Arts. One had better make his fingers adapt themselves to the existing condition gradually and quickly. After making practice a little turpentine oil or rheumatism oil can be used to rub one's fingers to quicken the circulation of the blood so as to protect his fingers. So a poem runs "Power originates from finger-insertion, Qi comes from Dantian. Inserting the rice at start. Turn to insert the sand at last. Bloody and swollen your fingers will be. Thousands of times need to have been done. Scrabs on your fingers are seen. Again insert them into iron-sand. Again and again you must break through brambles and thorns. Your fingers and skins will be bloody. If your fingers' scabs are becoming very thick, you are said to have mastered the Arts. A hole you can chisel in the wall, for your fingers are like an iron-fork. "

3. Key to the Exercise: the Shaolin Master says that the training method is of little difficulty. That is the basic skill of Pressing Acupoints and Removing Bones. After accomplishment it is quite accessible to learn the Pressing Acupoints and through which the second step would have been acquired. The trainee had better choose a case, made of elm or ju-

130

jube, about 2 feet square, 1 foot in height. The yellow bean or rice can be used to fill in the case. It has proved that one's fingers are as hard as iron if he is able to practise inserting his hands into the case for one hour. - After training one can wash his hands with Qing Yan and Di Gu Pi simmered in the water and sterilized. Please remember it.

Removing Mountain Arts

First get a wood-stake, about three metres long. Sharpen its end and bury more than half length of it into the earth and make the stake stand firm. Then try your best to pull it up with your thumb, forefinger and middle finger. At the start you may get no result, just like a dwarf removing a mountain. Keep on making practice. You may strengthen your waist force day after day. And the stake can be lifted up slowly. You have achieved the Arts when the stake can be completely pulled out by you. While training you had better concentrate on yourself and gather your energy together to lift it up without shaking the stake. After having pulled out the wood stake, you can use an iron-stake instead. Practise it in the same way until you can lift it out at will (Fig. 37).

Brief Introduction

1. Removing-Mountain Arts is one of the hard and external-strong Arts in the seventy-two consummate skills of internal and external Gongfu which the Shaolin Temple has inherited secretly. It belongs to
132

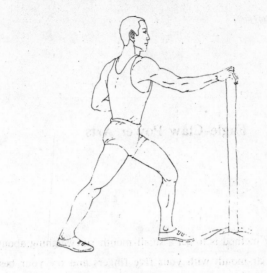

Fig. 37

that of Yang Gang character. This is a specific exercise of one's fingers.

2. Key to the Exercise : the Shaolin Master says that it is a Lifting Skill. One can use the magical force of his wrist to defeat an opponent. When successful , one's Yang Gang Energy make himself strong enough to defeat an opponent without touching the opponent's body , just like that of the Eagle-Claw Arts. After having mastered this Yin Rou Skill , one is said to be successful.

THIRTY-EIGHTH

Eagle-Claw Power Arts

The training method is to get a small-mouth jar, weighing about 10 catties. Take the jar-mouth with your five fingers and try your best to lift it up. At the start you may not lift it up for its surface is smooth. - Several months later you can lift it up and down at ease. Then every week, a bowl of silkworm droppings can be put into the jar for the practice of lifting until it is full up. After this, use iron-sand and then iron-slabs as the further step of practising. Now, if you are able to lift up the jar with iron slabs inside, you have mastered the Arts of Eagle-Claw Power. Then, turn to practise this skill barehanded, i. e. posturing to take a jar from the sunlight with your five fingers every early morning. If you make Qi follow your mind and make fingers to exert power, you have accomplished the Yin-Rou Arts of the Eagle-Claw Power (Fig. 38).

Brief Introduction

1. Eagle-Claw Power Arts, also called Dragon-Claw Arts, is one of

134

Fig. 38

the hard and soft Arts in the seventy-two consummate skills of internal and external Gongfu which the Shaolin Temple has inherited secretly. It belongs to both of Gang character and Yin Rou character, and the integration of Yin and Yang. This is a specific exercise of one's fingers.

2. There are two parts in the Eagle-Claw Power Arts: Gang Energy and Rou Energy. They are connected with each other. Gang Energy is the foundation of Rou Energy, but it develops under the support of Rou Energy. That is to say, if one masters Rou Energy skillfully without Gang Energy, there is no result. Without Rou Energy one is lacking of

135

flexible changes even if his Gang Energy achieves the highest peak. So Gang and Rou Energy are a unity of opposites, not a single one of them can be dispensed with.

3. Key to the Exercise: the Shaolin Master says that after having been versed in this Arts, one can attack any opponent as if he kills his opponent with a sharp knife. The internal organs of his opponent seems to have been stabbed. The strong fingers are of Yang Gang character. If one grasps nothing with his fingers, the energy he has belongs to that of Yin Rou Energy. Because of the mutual promotion and mutual restraint between one's Yin and Yang, he has usually to acquire his Yang first and then the Yin. To lay equally the stress on the Hardness and Softhess, one can get the Softness to dwell in Hardness. To grasp something means to practise the Hardness Energy. To grasp nothing means to assume the grasping of something in the air, the purpose of which is to withhold the Yang Gang Energy and produce the Yin Rou Energy. If one stretches his hands to make grasping from the sky after he completely mastered the Yin Energy, the bird in the air will be shot down. Take his action similarly toward a horse at a distance, he is able to pull it back. Grasping his opponent's acupoint, one immediately beats down his opponent. After having been good at Yang Gang Energy without Yin Rou, one can give his opponents a good beating, but not a deadly blow, for Yang Gang Energy without Yin Rou Energy is inferior to the Single-Finger Hand Stand, Cinnabar Palm and Yin Fist Arts. If the practice of this Arts is given up halfway, one's five fingers might retain to be hook-like and they will fail to respond to the medical treatment. Yin Rou Energy refers to that of concentrating on oneself and drawing one's Qi back.

Key-Fingers Arts

At first close your middle and index fingers, bend them and also bend your thumb. The tip of the thumb lies between the tips of your middle and index fingers. Make your three fingers to form a circle tightly and your palm is hollow (Fig. 39—1).

Now exert strong force to pinch each other tightly , for half an hour. Then take a rest and pinch each other again. Every day whenever you are free , try your best to practise   this skill. While doing pinching you should direct the total energy of your

Fig. 39-1

137

arms to the tips of your three fingers and concentrate your mind upon the practice. After one year take a hard wood plank about one inch in thickness and place it between the above said your three fingers. After having penetrated the plank with your finger or fingers, you have get the initial result. But, it takes one or two years for you to get the result. Then get an iron plate for making the same practice. If you can pinch it to have a deeply sunken curvature, you will have achieved this Arts (Fig. 39—2).

Fig. 39-2

Brief Introduction

1. Key-Fingers Arts is one of the soft and internal-strong Arts in the seventy-two consummate skills of internal and external Gongfu which the Shaolin Temple has inherited secretly. It belongs to both of Yin Rou Energy and Yang Gang Power. This is a specific exercise of one's fingers.

2. Key to the Exercise; the Shaolin Master says that this skill is very much similar to the Eagle-Claw Power and Ponit-Stone Arts. But it is a little different from the Eagle-Claw Power and Ponit-Stone Arts. Key-Fingers Arts is that of practising the skill of pinching. To accomplish this Arts, one may spend four or five years. One had better practise it with his left hand. It was said that a Buddhist monk in the Shaolin Temple accidentally created this Arts. He practised penmanship assiduously every day. He held the Chinese writing brush with his three fingers and poured a few taels of lead into the hollow his writing-brush holder in order to make the strokes of the Chinese character vigorous and strong. He did it for twenty years. At last he won the fame for his penmanship and simultaneously mastered and invented this Arts. But he did not know about it. One day he played with his friend and accidentally kneaded his friend with his fingers. His friend cried out at the top of his voice and was found to have been injured. People regarded that his way of writing was a model which leads to the practising of martial Arts and began to practise this skill from then on.

Single-Finger Hand Stand Arts

At the beginning hang an iron hammer at the doorway and hit it every day with a single finger while coming and going. At the start the iron hammer will not sway. Afterwards it can be made to sway a little away. Then move yourself backward gradually to leave a distance between you and the hammer. If you needn't touch the hammer, i. e. just point your finger at the hammer and make the hammer sway, you have got the initial result. Now place a few lighted candles in the courtyard at midnight and stand at some distance in front of them and point at them one by one with your finger. At the start the flame just sways slightly. - Day by day as soon as the candles are pointed at, the light of them will be extinguished at once, just like that the lights are put out by a fan. This is the second step of success. Now make a piece of paper shaped like a cylinder and put the lighted candles inside the cylinder. Again try to practise this Arts. The third step will be successful if your finger points at the candle through the paper cylinder and put out its light without breaking the paper. Finally get a piece of glass to stand in front of the

140

lighted candles. If you are able to put out the light without breaking the glass, you have reached the zenith (Fig. 40).

Fig. 40

Brief Introduction

1. Single-Finger Hand Stand Arts is one of the soft and internal-strong Arts in the seventy-two consummate skills of internal and external Gongfu which the Shaolin Temple has inherited secretly. It belongs to that of one's Yin Rou Energy.

141

2. Single-Finger Hand Stand Arts is to direct one's whole energy to a single finger of his (generally the forefinger). One can make this practice with the method of Up-Side-Down-Standing. In the actual fighting the might of Single-Finger Hand Stand Arts is beyond description. - Master Hai Deng, a master-hand in the modern Shaolin School, pointed out that Single-Finger Hand Stand Arts reached the highest peak of Wushu. Once he inserted his finger through a two-layered sand-bag (the inner-layer is made of canvas; the other is made of white cloth), filled with sand weighing 200 catties.

3. Key to the Exercise: the Shaolin Master says that it is an exercise of one's single finger. The famous Shaolin Master Qi Hei-Zi, in the Southern China, practised the Arts for about forty years. In the Arts of a single finger the people in the world are no match for him. One should spend ten years in practising this Arts. Comparing with the Red Cinnabar-Palm, Black Cinnabar-Palm and Five-Poison Hands, this Arts takes the lead. But the trainee must persevere in practising this skill.

Picking-Up Flower Arts

At first, you needn't use any apparatus. Close your middle and index fingers tightly and press your thumb on them and make them touch each other on three finger-sides. Then do screw turnings around to make pickings in and out for the same number of times. Make practices in this way every day as many times as possible. Take a rest if you get tired. You can practise this skill at any time and at any where without being easily noticed. Stick to the practice for one year and your fingers will be very tough. Now, get three very big and round grains of soybean, and make an effort to pick them in and out with the above said steeled thumb, middle and index fingers. At first you may not be able to hold the three grains together to turn screw pickings. One month later, you will get used to doing this. Renew the soybeans one or two times every day. The first step of success is that you can pick up the three grains of soybean and crush them into pieces at the first turning. Then, use three small pieces of yellow stone instead of three grains of soybean. Only when you can pick them up and crush them into pieces in the above-said

143

way, will you be said to have made successes in this Arts. You must spend five years in practising the skill(Fig. 41).

Brief Introduction

1. Picking Up Flower Arts is one of the soft and external-strong Arts in the seventy-two consummate skills of internal and external Gongfu which the Shaolin Temple has inherited secretly. It belongs to that of Yin Rou Energy. This is a specific exercise of the fingers.

Fig. 41

2. Key to the Exercise : the Shaolin Master says that this is a specific exercise of fingers' picking ability. The finger is a minor part of the body and is not as strong as the fist or palm. Therefore it is rather difficult for a learner to practise the fingers' skill. But if he sticks to the practice he will certainly achieve this skill. After accomplishment he can kill a person if his fingers touch the latter's body. It is similar to the Saddle Arts or Guan Yin Palms Arts ,etc.

FORTY-SECOND

Centipede-Leaping Arts

First, support your body with both palms and feet, the chest being two or three inches above the ground. This posture is just like "Push-Up" in the modern gymnastics. Raise the middle part of your body posturing a bow-like position. There and then, apply force to press the ground with your palms and with your feet. Make a strong stamp to make leaping forward. Thus you will leap in the air to a distant ground. But, take care to keep the bow-like posture with your body being two or three inches above the ground. After having acquired this leaping skill, strive to practise the skill with your fists to take the place of your two palms. Then, use five fingers, three fingers, two fingers, finally one finger. Two feet can be reduced to one foot. When you are able to leap forward and backward in this way at ease you will have won great successes (Fig. 42).

Brief Introduction
1. Centipede-Leaping Arts is one of the hard and external-strong

145

Fig. 42

Arts in the seventy-two consummate skills of internal and external Gongfu which the Shaolin Temple has inherited secretly. It belongs to that of Yang Gang character and is an exercise of fingers and feet.

2. Centipede-Leaping Arts, formerly called "Centipede-Spring", "Bending-Body Spring" and "Snake-Wriggling Skill", is a common skill in the case of Ground Boxing, Night-Combating Skill and Dramatic Wushu. Centipede-Leaping Arts is divided into Centipede Vertical Leaping Arts (Note: the skill calls for leaping up several times on each occasion and then returning to the original place in turn), Centipede Horizontal Leaping Arts (Note: Leaping sideway several times on each occasion,

146

then leaping back along the original route), Centipede Swirling Leaping Arts (Note: Leaping up with hands turning to the left and feet turning toward the right, forming a screw leaping on the spot), and Centipede Spring Arts (Note: Take the waist as a pivot and make handstand with press, i. e. with both arms resting on the ground and both feet held high straight upward in the air. On the contrary, feet on the ground and arms straight upward.) The main training goal is to improve the ability of leaping and the power of fingers and toes, so that the movement of the various parts of the body will be harmonious. Do remember: while leaping the waist and the abdomen must be towering up.

3. Key to the Exercise: the Shaolin Master says that it is indispensable for the Night-Fighter to learn this skill. It is an excellent Gongfu for steeling hands and feet. It concurrently includes the training of leaping skill. After having accomplished it, while coming across an opponent, not only can you defeat him, but also you can make escape from him with the help of leaping ability. In the case of fighting, you can lie on the ground and crawl and avoid being found. Moreover, you can make a sudden attack against your opponent.

Lying-Tiger Arts

While training, do push-up exercise. Press your palms on the ground on a level with your shoulders. Stretch your feet straight with feet-toes touching the ground, thus supporting your body to rise to about one foot high above the ground. Then, take advantage of a favourable position to lean forward. Withdraw your buttocks backward making your body lean backward to three inches above the ground. Do this exercise again and again until you are feeling completely exhausted. From A to Z, all the other parts of your body are supported in the air with the exception of your palms and foot toes. At the start, you may get tired after having done it for two or three times. As time goes on, the training times should be increased. One year later, in the course of training, you will feel at ease. The next step is to use your fists instead of your palms to practise the skill. After several months of training, use three fingers instead of your fists with the middle and index fingers in front and the thumb in the rear looking like the form of a mouse-claw. Afterwards, use a single foot-toe to support your body and lean forward and backward as

148

before. At last, bind a large stone slab on your back to do the same exercise. If the weight of the stone slab increases to a hundred catties, you are considered to have made a great success (Fig. 43).

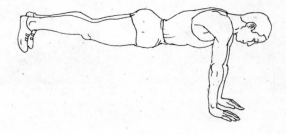

Fig. 43

Brief Introduction

1. Lying-Tiger Arts is one of the hard and external-strong Arts in the seventy-two consummate skills of internal and external Gongfu which the Shaolin Temple has inherited. It belongs to that of Yang Gang character. It is an exercise of training fingers and feet toes. It is also called Sleeping Gong Arts or Cat Gong Arts.

2. Key to the Exercise: the Shaolin Master says that it is an exercise of training fingers and feet. The power of one's fingers and toes will be able to sustain more than thousands of catties. And the touching of

149

trained fingers and toes as mentioned above will mean to have the same effect of a spear's piercing or a knife's killing.

Tortoise-Back Arts

Before getting up every morning, sit cross-legged, close your eyes to make your mind calm down and concentrate your attention to nourish your Qi. Then, press your hands on your back waist and massage toward inside for thirty-six times, and then turn to massage toward outside for thirty-six times too. It means One-Turn of the exercise. After One Turn, press your thumb on the first joints of the middle and index fingers and knock at the waist with the projecting bones of the second joints. Knock at it then with both hands for three hundred and sixty times. After having finished knocking, return to make massages. And after massaging, turn to make knocking again. You must finish the process of massaging and knocking three times every day. While doing it, bear the number of times in mind. Don't make a mistake. To count the number may help you to concentrate upon your training. That means the eyes watch the nose and the nose watches the heart. After one year, you will make you kidney healthy. Then, make an effort to practise the Hammer Technique. A softwood hammer takes the place of the fist. It is better for the handle of the hammer to be made of rattan. While training, direct your Qi to the waist-back and beat the waist-back with the hammer from up to down and from left to right. At first, make beating gently. Thereafter, gradually beat the waist-back more heavily. At ordinary times, you should wear tight an iron sleeveless vest woven with iron rings of the size of a silver dollar coin, which is called a half suit of armour by the Southerners. The iron vest is worn on the upper part of your body and buttoned in front of the chest and shoulders with strings. When lying, you are to lie on your back on a hard wood board. When training, take off the vest and put it on after training. The weight of the iron vest should be from light to heavy. While beating, use the lighter and softer wood hammer first and then use the harder and heavier wood hammer until an iron hammer may be used to take the wood hammer's place. Step by step, when you can stand the beating of the waist with a big iron hammer without feeling painful, you will be taken to have made a big accomplishment (Fig. 44).

Brief Introduction

1. Tortoise-Back Arts is one of the hard and external-strong Arts in the seventy-two consummate skills of internal and external Gongfu which the Shaolin Temple has inherited secretly. It belongs to that of Yang Gang character and is an exercise of training the back and kidney.

2. Key to the Exercise: the Shaolin Master says that it is an exercise of training the back, the same type as that of the Cloth-Bag and Iron-Cow Arts. The skill is just for self-defence only. It is more efficient to practise the upper back for its bones are closely lined together and is difficult to practise the lower back for its bones between two kidneys are soft and gentle. So if you want to master the Tortoise-Back Arts, you

152

Fig. 44

should practise it assiduously and diligently. The Arts includes the training of the trunk of a body from the neck to the anus. If you want to strengthen your waist, you have to direct your energy (Qi) to your back. While training, you should concentrate on gathering your energy and then start to beat the waist. If you lack this skill, you would not be able to achieve the Arts. If you practise and combine Tortoise-Back Arts with Iron-Head Arts, Iron-Clothes Arts and Iron-Cow Arts, none of any other skills can defeat you except the Soft Arts, such as Single-Finger Hand Stand Arts, Cinnabar Palms and Yin Fist Arts. It is really an excellent skill for self-defence. The internal Gong in Shaolin Temple is not inferior to the Qi of Wudan School.

153

Door-Crotch Arts

Sit cross-legged. Concentrate your attention upon your mind which is not to be soiled by a speck of dust and cast away any trouble. Then, direct the whole energy downward to Dantian and make great efforts to lift Qi up, thus making the Qi travel up and down again and again. Do in this way several times every day. Don't make haste, otherwise, you will be too tired to get a good result. At the very start, you may not realize the improving of your health. After a long-run exercise of directing Qi to Dantian, you must feel that the lower part of your trunk is becoming strong and tough. Now you have got the first-step success. Again, sit cross-legged. Lift your Qi and pat the hips with full-of -Qi palms light-ly. At first, the patting may cause unbearable pain. Day after day, through directing Qi to Dantian, you will feel painless. This is the sec-ond-step success. Again, apply force to beat the hips with fists. If you be-come resistant to fist beating, you have got the third-step success. Then, solwly stand up. If you can still stand the beating with fists as rapidly as the storm falling, you are taken to have finished the accomplishment of

154

this Arts(Fig. 45).

Fig. 45

Brief Introduction

1. Door-Crotch Arts, also called Golden Cicada Arts, is one of the
soft and external-strong Arts in the seventy-two consummate skills of
internal and external Gongfu which the Shaolin Temple has inherited secretly. It belongs to that of Yin Rou character. This is an exercise of
training the kidney.

2. Kidney is the main excretory organ of a human body. It belongs

to Water In Five Elements. [1] The common saying goes: "Kidney moving is as fast as that of the wind". The Boxing Symposium in respect of the Shaolin Temple has it that Heaven and Earth are at war (You fight with the other). The cloud shelters the Sun and the Moon (Beat the other's eyes with your hands). While combating against each other, you must first close the Five Elements to protect the kidney. Therefore, practising the skill of Door-Crotch Arts is valued for its merits in the case of actual fighting.

3. Key to the Exercise: the Shaolin Master says that it is very difficult to practise this Arts for it includes the main Gong. The Arts serves to enable the hips to be trained strong and tough.

---

[1]   Five Elements (Wuxing): Wood, Fire, Earth, Metal and Water are the five essential substances that constitute the material world and are also indispensable to the daily life of human beings. They are interrelated through mutual-production and mutual-conquest (checking), and under go endless changes and movement.

——**Elementary Chinese Medicine**

Iron-Cow Arts

First, direct Qi to the abdomen, knock at it with finger joints slightly for several times a day. When taking a rest, apply force to massage it with palms. From day to day, the skin and muscle of your abdomen will be strong and tough. Thereafter, beat it with your fist for many times a day. At first, you may feel a dull pain. Day by day. you will feel well even if you exert force to beat it heavily. Then, use a wood hammer instead of the fist. Later on, use an iron hammer instead of a wood one. At the beginning of beating with an iron hammer, the sound of beating is just like the droning of a tree falling. The sound will be loud and clear when you have made progress in practising. Finally, the sound can be heard like the clanging of metal and stone, which is a symbol of approaching the final stage of achievement. Now, place a large stone slab on your abdomen before going to bed and take it away after getting up. - Comparatively speaking, it is more strenous for you to bear the weight of a large stone. Only when you can sleep soundly with a stone slab of 180 catties in weight on your stomach, can you be considered to have made the highest achievement of this Arts(Fig. 46).

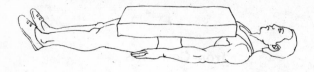

Fig. 46

Brief Introduction

1. Iron-Cow Arts is one of the hard and external-strong Arts in the seventy-two consummate skills of internal and external Gongfu which the Shaolin Temple has inherited secretly. It belongs to that of Yang Gang character. It is a specific exercise of training the abdomen.

2. Through practising this Arts, you may arrive at the standard of "Qi deposites in Dantian", and make the abdomen strengthened and re-sistent. This kind of elasticity can bear to a certain extent the heavy beating and pressing.

3. Key to the Exercise: the Shaolin Master says that the training process of this Arts is similar to that of the Cloth-Bag Arts, but there lies the difference between opening and closing the mouth. It is an Arts for self-defence and not for making an attack. If your opponent attacks you with his fist or a weapon, his fist must be injured and the weapon will be broken. You will be invincible. What is the difference between the skill of Opening Mouth and that of Closing Mouth after all? While applying

158

force, if you can still talk with the others, it is called Opening Mouth Iron-Cow Arts, which is better than Closing Mouth Iron-Cow Arts. The successful completion of practising this Arts will have a result that you are resistant to the attack made by the use of a spear or a sword. But it should avoid the attack of an Immortal Palm Arts.

Gunny-Bag Arts

At the beginning, sit cross-legged every day, and direct your Qi into your abdomen. Then massage in the same direction its left side and right side for thirty-six times each time with your hands. Again, massage its left side towards its right side and then rub its right side towards its left side. At last, exhale your Qi to restore it to its original condition. Lastly, massage it with your two hands in the same way for thirty-six times. - Stick to practice in this way for one or two years and your abdomen will become as soft as cotton. At this time if you direct your Qi to it, it will seem to be as hard as iron. Now, use a big piece of canvas cloth to serve as a stake on which is set up horizontally a wood stick. Sustain the end of the horizontal stick with your abdomen and concentrate your attention upon lifting your Qi up. Thus, make the abdomen wrap the end of the stick. Drag the stick backward. At first, the stick may easily fall down. After training for a long time, the end of this stick will be seen to have been suck by your abdomen, just like its taking root in your abdomen. It is impossible now to pull the stick out of your abdomen even if you apply great force to do it, for the stick has been firmly wrapped by your abdomen. You have made a great achievement in the Arts now. Besides, should you regulate your Qi in you abdomen, the sucked stick will be forced to fly out directly. If your opponent thrusts out his fist to attack your abdomen, he will find that his fist is deeply sucked and there is no possibility of its being pulled out again. Moreover, he will feel that his fist has been shackled with an unbearble pain. Even an iron stick can not hurt your abdomen either(Fig47).

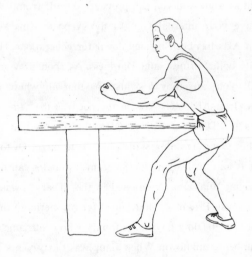

Fig. 47

Brief Introduction

1. Gunny-Bag Arts is one of the soft and internal-strong Arts in the seventy-two consummate skills of internal and external-Gngfu which the Shaolin Temple has inherited secretly. It belongs to both the Yin Rou character and Yang Gang Energy. It is a specific exercise of training the abdomen.

2. Cloth-Bag Arts lays stress on getting rid of the stale and taking in the fresh, and Qi travels to Dantian to fill the inner-Qi of the abdomen-. After a long-run exercise the abdomen will become both as soft as cotton and as hard as iron. And you can prevent yourself from being beaten and can improve your internal Gongfu too. A poem runs as follows: "Iron-abdomen Arts has been handed down for generations. How excellent it is for its both Softness and Hardness. As soon as you have acquired this skill, you can enjoy a sightseeing tour anywhere within the paradise. (Note: Iron-Abdomen Arts in the poem is the same as that of Cloth-Bag Arts)." Diary of a Qing Official "records that in Shaolin Temple there lies Gong-Training skill, which is to direct Qi to the muscles to become as hard as leather. The so-trained muscles can not be hurt by a sword. Huang Yuanxing, mentioned in the "Diary", was a gallant man in Huai(Jiangsu Province) and famed for his merits in the village. He took in and brought up a boy in his family whose surname was Jiang, his full name being unknown. When Jiang was thirty years old he became very strong. He could carry a large piece of stone on his back and make a rapid walk hundreds of steps away. There was a very ponderous cart in a hall. Two cows could barely draw it. Jiang sat silently by the side of the cart, his abdomen leaving uncovered, and having a natural breath. In a few minutes, he rose slightly for several times, directed Qi to

162

his arms which gave forth a rustling and to his abdomen which swelled gradually. About half an hour later, he stood up and got a sharp pointed and bright sword, three feet in length. He held its handle to support the cart and sustained the pointed-end of the sword with his abdomen. Then he inclined forward with his hands held at his back and made an endeavour to make its pointed-end push into his abdomen. The cart was made to circle seven or eight rounds. Then he released the sword. His abdomen still lay projecting without any sign of having been hurt. "

3. Key to the Exercise: the Shaolin master says that it does not mean to use the gunny-bags to practise this Arts. This Arts lays emphasis on attaining the soft Gong of the abdomen which is to be just like the gunny-bag of Buddha Maitreya, whose gunny bag contains Hun Yuan Qi for the defence of any kind of attack. The Gunny-Bag Arts means the co-operation of Yin and Yang, and its softness dwells in its hardness. - There is no comparison between the Gunny Bag Arts and the Iron-Cow Arts. The latter dwells only its Yang Gang Energy. One must seriously spend ten years to attain this Arts.

Inhaling-Yin Arts

Calm down, concentrate your mind which is not to be soiled by a speck of dust and cast away any worldly trouble. Direct your whole Qi to be deposited in your Dantian and make every effort instantly to lift up the Qi, and make the Qi go up and down in circulation. Practise in this way several times every day. Don't make haste otherwise you will be too tired to get the result. At the start, you may not feel your health improving, and day by day, your scrotum will swell like a ball while directing Qi to your Dantian. Your testis will become active while lifting the Qi up. Only when your testis is drawn up to your abdomen through the process of lifting up the Qi, leaving the scrotum out, keeping your testis within your abdomen, can you protect your testis from its being caught (Fig. 48).

Brief Introduction

1. Inhaling-Yin Arts, also called Drawing-Yang Arts, is one of the soft and internal arts in the seventy-two consummate skills of internal

164

and external Gongfu which the Shaolin
Temple has inherited secrethy. It belongs
to that of Yin Rou Energy. This is a specific exercise of training the human
crotch.

2. Inhaling-Yin Arts is to practise
the skill of drawing testis to abdomen. As
the crotch is an upmost important and
delicate physical part of the body of a
male, it has a network of nerve tissues
and is therefore very sensitive. Again, a
mere tempting upon the testis will cause
an unbearable pain or even bleeding. Also
a slight striking upon the testis may give
rise to serious cases of stifling, fainting
and heart failure. With the lapse of time
the after-math will be the chronic disease
of the weaken sexual functioning and the
feeling of pain. Therefore, you as well as

Fig. 18

anybody have to practise this Arts. The lifting on purpose of the scrotum
coupled at the same time with drawing of the anus inward will make the
scrotum shrink tightly and become strong, so that in the course of doing
exercise, it will not be moving.

3. Key to the Exercise: the Shaolin Master says that the essence of
the training of this skill means to direct Qi and draw the testis to the abdomen, and prevent it from being attacked from outside. Actually it is
different from the Internal Gong. The latter refers to get the real Qi to

165

fill the limbs, the whole body, all channels and all acupoints in order to resist fire, water, cold and heat. No doubt, inhaling-Yin Arts is one of the soft Gong. In short, by depositing Qi in the scrotum or drawing Qi out of the scrotum, the scrotum can be strong and stiff enough to give protection to the testis. It is an art of directing Qi to the abdomen for self defence.

Soft-Bone Arts

It is better to begin with leg kicking. The proverb runs: "Boxing without leg kicking, you will be a harumscarum all your life". What is the meaning of leg kicking? It means kicking with a single leg. While kicking, the sitting leg is to stand erect and the kicking leg is to be stretched very straight. Kick as high as possible. The boxer says: "The leg of 'Lower-Kicking' (Tan Tui)is not to be held higher than the height of the knee. Normally the kicking leg should kick upward briskly and fall rapidly. " The pass standard is kicking overhead. In the case of the training of leg kicking, kick with either leg by turns for hundreds of times in one course every morning and every evening. After half-a-year practice of leg kicking, start to practise "Facing-Sky Kicking". It means to stand erect on one leg, and raise the other leg stretched-straight from the front part of your body with your hand and make it close to your rib and upward to let the bottom of your leg face the sky. Practise in this way by turns. A few months later, make every endeavour to practise the skill of One-Line Legs Arts. There are two sorts of skill in this Arts: Horizontal

167

One-Line Legs means to stretch the legs toward left and right respectively resulting in your sitting on the flat ground with your legs forming one straight line lying close to the ground; Vertical One-Line Legs means to stretch your legs toward the front and the rear. Stretch the left leg toward the front and the right leg towards the rear. Both legs lie close on the ground forming a straight line, then stretch your legs in the reverse way. All the above practice lay emphasis on the training of legs (Fig. 49-1). But how to practise the art of training the waist? For the first course, begin with the practice of "A Cat Straightens Its Waist", "An Overlord Lifts High a Tripod", "An Immortal Bows With Hands Folded In Front", "Stand At Attention With Both Feet Erect". For the second step hold your hands above your head with fingers crossed. Stand erect with both legs straight. Bend the upper part of your body till the palms of your hands touch the ground and your head and your shoulder should be in the same level. After a quarter of an hour, retrieve your body and have a rest. After having made successes in practising this skill, turn to practise the art of Overturning, common-

Fig. 49-1

ly called "Ao Yuan Bao". Bend your waist backward with your fists

168

stretched to touch the ground until your trunk is shaped like the arched span of a bridge. Then, again practise the skill of Body Folding To Left and Right, thus making your body to be soft, and your waist and legs will become active and flexible. When lying, you can twist your body around to be like a ring easily. The power of stretching and bending of your body certainly becomes stronger than that of the others. And it is a very favourable condition for you to learn on apparatus (Fig. 49—2).

Fig. 49-2

Brief Introduction

1. Soft-Bones Arts is one of the soft and internal arts in the seventy-two consummate skills of internal and external Gongfu which the Shaolin Temple has inherited secretly. It belongs to that of main Gong of "Internal Strong". It is an exercise of training one's waist and legs.

2. "Boxing Illustration" says that broad shoulder and slim waist re-

169

sult from a long-term training. He who has both the skill of inhaling Qi to the abdomen and soft waist must be versed in boxing. If he can crawl like a looper, it means that his hands and feet will be able to stretch, shrink, bend, twist, rise and fall freely and easily to link the various organs co-ordinately so as to direct his Qi to Dantian. When practising Gong, his waist must be kept as soft as cotton so as to take an ideal position and make use of the soft Gong to deal with the case. It says again: "The waist is the axis of one's body. It must be flexible and energetic, for the power originates from it and Qi is also directed by it. If one crooks his waist stiffly, he may not be able to direct Qi and his upper body and lower body can not be linked co-ordinately. The Boxing Proverb goes: "Qi is the source of the waist", "Strong waist makes the kidney and heart strong"; "Strong kidney makes the waist active"; "Boxing without a lively waist means that the boxer's skill is not high"; "Feet are wheels. Waist is a pivot. Take care of the waist at any moment", etc. All these indicate that the waist plays a significant role in the Shaolin Wushu.

3. It is very obvious that the waist is a determining factor in the Shaolin Wushu. For instance, the Shaolin Foundemental Wushu has it: Stand in left(right) bow-shaped step, thrust right (left) fist. "As long as we twist our waist toward the left (right), we can bring waist muscles into full play and take a favourable position to make us apply total force to go through our shoulders or our legs while boxing. The proverb runs; "Flow through the shoulders, hurry to the elbows and reach the hands". In free combating, Shaolin Wushu will play as follows. If your opponent directly thrusts out his fist to attack your chest, you can twist slightly your waist to change your trunk's position and your opponent will fail in

his attacking. And, if you want to make a counter-attack, you need not lunge forward. Twist back your waist and you will succeed in directly beating him. This Arts means a practical application of the art of training your trunk to deal with combating. So the Boxing Guide says: "Movement and Calmness belong to one's waist. One will suffer from sickness if he does not take a good care of his waist. If you are lacking strength, do not know how to take advantage of the favourable position and are not able to move around flexiblely, you will not be able to take the upper hand in the case of combating even though you are on the alert". That is the reason why it is necessary for you to be good at offence and defence. In short, it is necessary for you to have a good command of both Gang and Rou.

4. "Eight Skill Arts" in Shaolin Wushu requires that on the one hand body skill should be "Waist Moves Like Snake Crawling". So the "Body Skill" calls for that the body must be flexible and changable. On the other hand, you should improve the pliability of your thoracic verte-bra and waist vertebra. The waist lies in the most flexible part of the body. It is the pivotal part of the upper and lower limbs, and is the " middle part" of Shaolin Three Parts (Hands and Elbows are the Upper-Part; Waist and Abdomen are the Middle Part; Legs and Feet are the Root-Part.)The waist in Shaolin Wushu is taken to be an important link for adapting to the changeable skill of Body Arts, regulating and co-ordi-nating the functions of the different organs, adjusting the body's centre of gravity and bring the strength into play as well. The waist must be very agile, harmonious, speedy and flexible. Through the practice of Rou-Bones Arts, you can improve the flexibility and elasticity of the waist, legs, joints and ligament, and can better control the muscles.

Therefore, the Boxing Illustration says; "The waist is the leading factor of Wushu. No wonder it is called the pivotal part of the trunk. "In short, the exercise of the waist plays the most important role in Wushu. There are two ways of training: One is that of projecting the waist with the buttocks overturning backward. The other is that of crooking the waist backward, the anus sinking down. The former is advocated by the Outer-School, the latter by the Inner-School. In my opinion, the learner must make use of his well-developed figure and do practice on the basis of his naturally inborn ability. Thus, in the course of practising no matter how the learner sits or squats his waist will be kept in the centre, i. e. directly under the hip. He is not to swing forward nor to turn to the left or to the right.

5. Key to the Exercise: the Shaolin Master says that the common saying about the Gongfu has it: Twisting Waist and Folding Legs means a kind of Soft Gong which the learners must practise, for the soft Gong makes the trainees be active and dexterous in the movement. Further-more, if he fills the boiled water into a wood tub covered with a piece of white cloth before training and in a few minutes it will become warm. Now he lies on his back over the tub so that the vapour of warm steam will go up to his waist. In this way he can make greater progress.

Iron-Broom Arts

Every day, stand in riding-horse stance. When getting tired, have a break. Then, practise again. At the start, need not spend too much time. By and by if you practise for about two hours without feeling tired, you are taken to have the first step success. The riding-horse stance advocates the steady body and firm steps. After a long-run exercise, the strength of your two legs will be invincible. Now, bury wood stakes at the doorway or at a distant place, and horizontally kick them with your legs continually. You can kick the stakes with a single leg or double legs. At first, your legs may be swollen, but after days of training, your legs' muscles will become tough without the feeling of pain. On account of your kicking the stakes may vibrate hard or be broken. Then, bury bigger stakes instead of the smaller one to make practice. After three years of training, your kicking can shake the branches of a big tree or break its trunk. If you can break the tree easily, you have made a big achievement of the Iron-Broom Arts (Fig. 50).

Fig. 50

Brief Introduction

1. Iron-Broom Arts, also called Iron-Legs Gong, is one of the hard and external-strong arts in the seventy-two consummate skills of internal and external Gongfu which the Shaolin Temple has inherited secretly. It belongs to that of Yang Gang character. It is a specific exercise of the legs.

2. The Boxing Guide says: "The legs sustain the whole body, bear the weight of the body and make the body stand firm like a mountain. The legs move like the rivers streaming, their motion being steady and smooth. If Qi does not float up, the body will remain standing erect". The beginner without the legs' Gongfu is often swayed by the "wind", just as the tree without the root. But in the case of a veteran, his every

174

action is rooted in his feet, comes from his legs, is mainly controlled by his waist and carried out by his fingers. It means a circulation of Qi from the feet to the legs and to the waist . So, that is a task of top priority to practise the Leg Skill. Again the Boxing Guide says : "The power to command the feet is also the meritorious service of the legs. The legs must be postured both to be hanging and shrinking and to be active and tough. It is better to take a posture to hide groin in the path to the waist with the apperance of a carpenter's square". A Boxing Proverb says : "Hands protecting oneself like a two-leafed door. Relying entirely on one's legs to beat the opponent". "To thrust fists amounts to thirty percent; to kick with legs to seventy percent. " " To beat the opponent with legs requires a series of kicking" etc. All the proverbs indicate that the legs play a considerable role in Shaolin Wushu. Again a poem runs : The front leg lies bowed. The back leg is a bowstring. The bow remains a bow. The bowstring is like a nail. The bow combines with the nail. The power hides inside. Steadiness and firmness are like a mountain. None of the forces can draw it. "

3. Five Key points must be made known in the skills of Shaolin Wushu. They are : Hand Skill, Eye Skill, Leg Skill, Body Skill, Step Skill. The Leg Skill indicates that, while defending or attacking, the boxer uses the tiptoes, the heel, the sole, the inner-thigh, the outer-thigh, the inner-shank and the outer-shank, etc. In the actual combat, how powerful it is for the boxer to use his leg skill properly. While fighting, the boxer gains more advantage to kick the legs of the opponent than to thrust his fists, for the leg is longer and more powerful than the arm and will not be easily noticed by the opponent. The "Arts of War" written by Sun-Zi, an ancient famous military scientist, says "Defeat your opponent by a sur-

175

prising attack. Attack wherever or whenever the enemy lies unpre-
pared. "Furthermore, the boxer can attack every part of the opponent's
body with his legs. In the upper part, he can beat the opponent at the
chest or the head. In the middle part, strike the opponent at the waist or
the abdomen. In the lower part, hit the enemy's legs and feet. The Leg
Skill is quite changable and the boxer always gains extra advantage
through leg kicking. The learner of Shaolin Wushu usually lays stress on
the training of legs and feet.

4. There are dozens of Leg Skills in Shaolin Wushu. They take
Springing, Juggling, Kicking, Point Kicking, Shoveling, Twinning, Inter-
locking, Hooking, etc. as the dominant factors. There are divisions of Inside Crescent Kick, Outside Kick, Back Kick, Up-Side-Down Kick, Front
Leg Sweep, Back Leg Sweep, Whirling Kick. All of them can combine
themselves with Leg Skills of Flying And Leaping, including Flying Feet
Kick, Slap Lotuts Kick, Arrow Spring Kick, Kick Sideways and Kick
Lower Legs With Toes Up along with the skills of Whirling Body including Whirling Kick, Whirling Wind Kick etc. All these skills can be put
into use according to one's choice. But if one didn't practise the leg skill
assiduously, his legs would have been powerless and slow, and he would
easily be hurt and beaten by the opponent. Therefore, every beginner
lays emphasis on the training of legs. The fundamental training method is
to do leg pressing and leg kicking and practise the "Soft-Bones Skill" to
improve the agility and flexibility of joints with the purpose of laying a
good foundation of leg kicking. In addition to these, one must strive to
practise the "Iron-Broom Arts", "Cypress-Tree Stakes Arts" etc. including the training of kicking Sand-Bag, sweeping the tree, so as to bring the
legs into powerful play and defeat the opponent.

5. Key to the Exercise: the Shaolin Master says that this Arts is one of the Gongfu in the legs training for the learner to make his leg strong and tough in order to sweep and beat the opponent. The skill requires the boxer to direct his whole energy to the legs as well as to the shanks. When the boxer comes under attack from all sides, he can sweep his opponents with legs and break their bones thoroughly. However, unless one perseveres in training, he can't hope to master it.

FIFTY-FIRST

Cypress-Stake Arts

The training course is quite easy. Bury less than half of a piece of cypress stake into the ground, kick it, stamp it hard. Imagine that the opponent is standing before you and you are kicking the lower part of his body. At the start, it may cause unbearable pain. Half a year later, the trainee will have a good command of the skill, and after one year, he will be invincible. Through the progress of directing his Qi to his feet he is able to make a very firm stand so that he can not be pushed away even by three men unless he lifts up his Qi. On kicking an opponent, he can immediately hit the opponent to the ground. This is the first step to success. Now, kick the Ji-Yong stone instead of the stake. This sort of stone can hardly be found. It was the stone put into use on the martial ground in the Qing Dynasty. It is about 500-700 catties in weight. The shape is upper-sharp, broad-bottom and rectangular. While kicking, he gets painful if his toes touch it. From day to day, he can kick the stone far away by a good kick. Now, he has reached the zenith (Fig. 51).

178

Fig. 51

Brief Introduction

1. Cypress-Stake Arts is one of the hard and external-strong arts in the seventy-two consummate skills of internal and external Gongfu which the Shaolin Temple has inherited secretly. It belongs to that of Yang Gang character. This is a specific exercise of the legs.

2. Key to the Exercise; the Shaolin Master says that it lays stress on the legs' power. The wrestlers usually practise this Arts and it is regarded as the fundamental skill by the boxers in the five Northern provinces of China. And he must practise it assiduously.

179

FIFTY-SECOND

Iron-Knee Arts

First, sit cross-legged, clench your fists and strike your knees for seventy-two times. After that, loose your fists and press your palms on your knees. Then massage them for thirty-six times from outward to inward and again from inward to outward. After massaging, strike them again. Do in this way for nine times. Before going to bed and getting up, practise this skill once again. One year later, your knee bones will be hard enough and then use 2 wood hammers instead of your fists. Each hammer are as big as the fist and in the shape of a ball or a drum, the handles of which should be made of rattan for the ratten is both soft and solid. Strike your knees with the two hammers simultanously for seventy-two times. Then, massage them for nine times as was previously done. After one year, your knees will be harder than ever. Now use two iron hammers to strike them. The size of the two iron hammers are the same as those of the wood hammers (1. 5 catties in weight each). You will accomplish this Arts after one year (Fig. 52).

180

Fig. 52

Brief Introduction

1. Iron-Knee Arts is one of the hard and external-strong arts in the seventy-two comsummate skills of internal and external Gongfu which the Shaolin Temple has inherited secretly. It belongs to that of Yang Gang character. This is a specific exercise of one's knees.

2. The Boxing Guide says: "The knees are doors of the lower part of the body." A boxer is to keep them close and is not to leave them open outward. On opening the knees, his feet-toes will certainly be opened so that the lower part of the body can not be shut tight. It is preferable to take the posture like squatting. Don't sit flatly or your legs and waist will not be sturdy. Again the Guide runs: "The function of the knees is

181

to make the feet steady and adjust the body's posture, for it's a pivot between the shank and thigh". One can direct the power of legs to the soles of feet so as to make the body stable and firm. The training method is to bend the knees but keep the knees' faces not to go in front of the toe tips so as to maintain the center of gravity. The back of knees is called "Knee Hollows". While treading in bow step, strectch one's "Knee Hollows" to send forth power. While squatting down, draw back one's Qi, so as not to fall down, but to easily launch an attack. The practical functioning of knees, which is similar to that of the elbows, includes the skills of Lifting, Squatting Down, Left Turning, Right Hanging, Front Defending, etc. But the beginner is unable to master it. Think that the cranes can stand on a single leg and remain tireless all day, because they apply force to the knees. Only when the learner makes every effort to learn from it, can he acquire the Arts. The proverb runs: "The leg does not lift the knee forcifully until it gets close to the opponent". After one's knee launches an attack toward the opponent's chest, one must withdraw the knee down to defend himself", "In a close fighting, it is a most effective to use the knees", etc. All these indicate that the knee plays an significant role in the Shaolin Wushu. So, the poem goes: "Hand catches hold of the groin, Feet strike knees, Raise knees to get close to the opponent's chest. Move elbows to defend the breast. Feet follow Hands. Hands downward follow the feet. Without the movement of steps, how can the hands be brought into play. "

3. In the Shaolin Boxing, the knee skill refers to that of using the knees to defend oneself and vanquishing the enemy. The main skills of the offensive and the defensive are to withhold the groin inside and raise the knee in order to gore, bump and shield, etc. The muscles include

182

musculus rectus femoris, muscle sartorius, tensor muscle of fassin lata, muscle pectineus, muscle adductor lonhus, etc. (especially, after the practising of "Iron-Knees"), all of which should have been strengthened. Meanwhile, with the help of Driving Force, one will be speedy, powerful and it's easy for him to strike the opponent away. While lifting the knees to make striking, the condyle of femur is always full of force. Thereby, the knees are quite beneficial to the actual combat. In addition, the attacking of knees now to left and now to the right means the mobile power of knees' joints. Although the power is not very mighty, it can weaken and diminish the opponent's attacking force. So the poem says, "To strike with knees at the vital parts of the body may cause death. It is just like a tiger shattering a flock of sheep. Both hands shelter the eyes just like the clouds covering the moon. Bending knees and kicking with legs give a deadly blow to the opponent. "

4. The knee is the juncture of thigh and shank. The knee joints consists inner-outer femur, joints of condyle, entocnemial condyle and kneecap, and it's also one of the complex joints in the body structure, and is the part to support one's whole body. Only one lays emphasis on the training of knee's joints at ordinary times, can one "handle a butcher's cleaver skillfuly" —— fight with the opponent with skill and at ease in the actual fighting. Through the training of "Iron-Knee Arts", one can strengthen the plibility of patellar ligament as well as the power of the waist, groin and thigh, including the hardness of condyle of femur, so as to direct the energy to the knee-tip and be beneficial to the training and fighting.

5. Key to the Exercise: the Shaolin Master says that the learner must be earnest to practise various skills. The more, the better. In respect

of the different parts of the body, the more parts he trains, the less he will be hurt. Sometimes he just uses the hidden and unnoticeable skill to conquer the enemy. After having acquired the Arts, his both knees are just like the iron-hammers. No matter whether he takes the offensive or defensive, he can make use of the knees, for instance, he can use the skills of Closing Knees and Seperating Knees. He can reach the highest degree of attainment after about two years' training.

Foot-Shooting Arts

It presents no difficulty. At dawn or dusk, while you take a walk, try to kick the bricks or stones with your toes. At the start, you may get painful but day by day the muscles of your toes will be both elastic and tough. And you must attempt to kick the bigger and bigger stones harder and harder. You may get an initial result only when you can kick the stone far away. Then, you make an effort to take an aim and kick the stones to a target. If you can hit the target, you will have come to a head (Fig. 53).

Brief Introduction

1. Foot-Shooting is one of the hard and external-strong arts in the seventy-two consummate skills of internal and external Gongfu which the Shaolin Temple has inherited secretly. It belongs to that of Yang Gang character. This is a specific exercise of the feet.

2. The Boxing Guide says: "The feet are the roots of the body. " If the roots are unsteady, the whole body must be weak, even though the

185

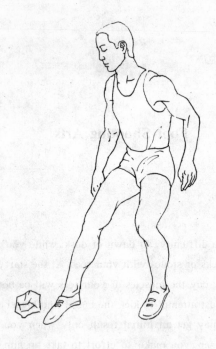

Fig. 53

other parts of the body are strong. Therefore, if your toes are "driven"
into the ground, your roots must be stable and firm. Don't rock forward
and backwards. Step back lightly. Step on speedily. Step forwards
briskly. And apply the other hundreds of footworks in accordance with
set rules. If so, your whole body will be full of vitality and invincible. "
Again, the Boxing Guide goes: The feet lie in the lowest part of the body
and are the roots of life. If the feet move, the body will move. If the feet
remain steady, the body will be in a pause. "So the learner should pay attention to where he is stepping and then he can make a plan of attacking

186

or defending, because the steps of feet can make one be quick, active and proper in fighting. Hence, "Feet are a decisive force". The Boxing Proverb goes: "Body follows the track of feets; Hands act harmoniously with the waist", "Feet for attacking distant opponents; knees for attacking nearby opponents", "Tread firm on the ground looking like a mountain and then mounting or stepping will come natural", etc. All these indicate that the feet play a considerably important part in the Shaolin Wushu. So, the poem says "The slightly horizontal front foot and the vertical back foot produce a T-Shape Energy. If the toes aren't raised, the heels cannot stand out. Make the toes snatch the ground like a tiger pouncing. Walking on stakes must be steady with the centre of the sole being hollow to appear like the wedge driven into the ground. Be dexterous and steady to enable the whole body to hold the centre of gravity. One should have a good command of Accuracy, Firmness, Hooking and Tripping with his feet."

3. "Eight Steps" in the Shaolin Wushu requires the feet stances to be "sticky" on the ground. The feet are the foundation of Stances and Footworks. Only when the foundation is firm, can one's footworks be in order so as to advance or retreat at his will. The Boxing Guide says: "Kicking force comes from the legs; Power originates from the heels. Through the exercise of 'Foot-Shooting', the flexibility of condylar articulation can be improved. The pouncing ability, sustaining force and kicking power of toes will certainly be beneficial to the boxing and sports as well." The poem says: "Kicking and trampling must not be let to lose the target. Heels determines where to make trampling. One's intention should not be detected by the opponent, and he must be nimble in changing stances."

187

4. Key to the Exercise : the Shaolin Master says that one can abrutly kick a stone to strike at the opponent in a distance in the actual fighting after accomplishment. When getting close to the opponent, one can kick the lower parts of the opponent's body. Moreover, he should take care to make the lower parts of his own safe.

Self-Hitting Arts

First, make a hard wood "Pai-Brick", one foot in length, six feet in width and one and a half inches in thickness. Hold the centre of the Pai-Brick and make a flank beating on each part of your body with its edges. First beat lightly and then heavier, the upper and lower arms now from the left and now from the right alternatively for a hundred times each time. Then, turn to beat the thigh and shank. While beating on the left leg, hold the Brick with the right hand and on the right leg with the left hand. After that, turn to beat on the chest and abdomen and lastly on the shoulder blades. In the morning and evening, beat the above-mentioned parts of the body one hundred times each time. After one year's training, you use the kiln brick instead of the wood brick. And half a year later, use the metal brick. You can accomplish this Arts after half a year's exercise by using a metal brick (Fig. 54).

Brief Introduction

1. Self-Beating is one of the hard and external-strong arts in the

189

seventy-two consummate skills of internal and external Gongfu which the Shaolin Temple has inherited secretly. It belongs to that of Yang Gang character. This is a specific exercise of one's resistant ability.

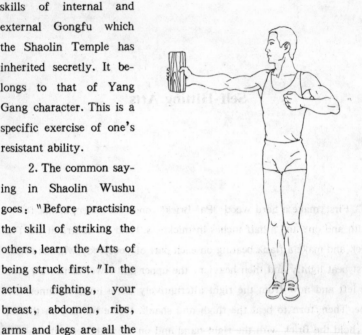

Fig. 54

2. The common saying in Shaolin Wushu goes: "Before practising the skill of striking the others, learn the Arts of being struck first." In the actual fighting, your breast, abdomen, ribs, arms and legs are all the parts prone to being injured by the opponent's violent action. Only when you practise the skill of "Self-Beating" successfully, can you be not easily defeated and be able to take time to direct your Qi to hit back the opponent at will. And through the exercise of "Self-Beating", you can improve the resistant ability of your internal organs and betray no fear in an hour of danger, i. e., you can bring your boxing skill into full play. In the Shaolin Wushu Circle, the common saying goes: "Inwardly, one should master a mouthful of Qi; Outwardly,

one must have the bones and skins trained. "To practise the "Self-Beating Arts" you should direct Dantian's Qi and combine it with the external bones, muscles and skins and move them in harmony in order to let the Mind direct Qi and Qi closely follow the Mind.

3. The ancient work, "Secret of Shaolin Wushu" states as follows: The method is to make a Rice Bag as an apparatus for beating. Sew a long round double-layered cloth bag, 1. 8 feet in length, 3 or 4 inches in diametre. Seal up one of its ends, and fill a half of the bag with rice. When it's half full, tie it tightly with a string. Its rest part is used for holding. The weight of rice in it is about two catties. For the old and the weak the weight of rice may be decreased according to their body condition. While beating with the rice bag, beat your body including the sides of hands and feet from left to right and from right to left alternately. (1)First, beat from inside of the left elbow to the left palm, then to the middle fingertip of the left hand. This is the inside-beating method of the left hand. (2) Again, beat in order from left elbow to the back of left hand, then to the middle fingertip of the left hand. This is the outside-beating method of the left hand. (3) Again, beat from the left armpit down to the small finger of the left hand. This is the lower beating method of the left hand. (4)Again, beat in order from the left shoulder to the thumb-side of the left hand. That's called above-beating method of the left hand. After finishing beating all sides of the left hand, continue to beat the left foot. (5)Beat from the left rib to the left lower abdomen, to the left thigh, and from the left wrist to the left shank, to the left knee, down to the left toes. This is the front-beating method of the left feet. (6)Again, beat from the left armpit to the left waist, to the left ankle, down to the left toes. This is the outside beating method of the left

foot. (7)Beat from the aorta bones of the left shoulder to the left side of the abdomen, then horizontally to the right side of the abdomen. Then, hold the rice bag with the left hand, beat the left abdomen from the right to the left, and cover the kidney with the right hand in order to prevent it from being injured. Then, beat from the left lower abdomen with the left hand, to inside of the left leg, to the left ankle, down to the left toes. This is the inside-beating method of the left leg. (8) Again, hold the rice bag over the head with both hands, and beat the left back blades twenty times. Then, hold the rice bag with the left hand and beat the left back blades from up to down. While beating down to the left waist, turn to beat the left thigh, to the calf, then down to the left heel. This is the back-beating method of the left foot. Then, continue to beat the four sides of the right hand and foot in the same way. Please remember.

While beating, you should beat from up to down in sequence. One beating follows the other. Do not miss beating a certain point or beat in the reverse direction. In case of missing the beating somewhere, never beat it again. When beating, you are to swallow a mouthful of Qi. And you should swallow sixteen mouthfuls of Qi in beating the left hand and foot and the right hand and foot. Altogether, you must swallow sixty-five mouthfuls of Qi. After one or two months, "Patrol-Hand Form" can be added and swallow four mouthfuls of Qi for this. And after another ten days, "Slanting-Lift Form" can be added and swallow six mouthfuls of Qi and three mouthfuls of Qi for Upright-Lift Form, i. e. nine mouthfuls of Qi for the above two forms. Ten days later again, add Xue-Gong Stance and swallow another three mouthfuls of Qi. Another ten days later, add Elbows-Arrangement and swallow six mouthfuls of Qi for it, i. e. twenty-two mouthfuls of Qi. 22 plus 65 mouthfuls of Qi equals to 87 in

192

all. Now, you have achieved this Arts.

4. Key to the Exercise: the Shaolin Master says that the skill seems to be the hard and external-strong arts but actually it is the soft and internal-strong arts. The training method is quite simple, but it makes the muscles stronger through beating them. Your muscles will become very tough and strong after accomplishment. And while beating, you should direct enough Qi to prevent the body from being injured. Meanwhile, you are to exhale first, and then direct the Qi again. You can also beat on the head to practise the skill of Head-Elbow. You have to spend two years in achieving this Arts. In the Northern Five provinces of China, this skill is regarded to be as important as the Soft-Bones Arts, and every beginner should practise this Arts but few boxers in the South go in for it. In the Shaolin Temple, this Arts keeps the same pace with the Beating Wooden Man Arts.

Somersault Turning Arts

First, practise the skill according to the position of Forward Somersault (Qiangbei). Swing one's right hand toward the left rib, let the right shoulder slightly touch the ground, overturn and stand up straight. That is called "Right-Forward-Somersault Position". Swing one's left hand toward the right rib, let the left shoulder slightly touch the ground, overturn and stand up straight. That is called "Left Forward-Somersault Position". It requires no effort for the trainee to practise the above two forms. The other forms are as follows. Forward-Somersault Position is to lean the head forward, overturn and stand up straight. This is commonly called "Turn a Somersault". Backward-Somersault Position is that the head leans backward, overturn and stand up straight. This is commonly called: "Counter-Somersault". Left-Somersault Position is to let the left shoulder lean leftward to make it slightly touch the ground, overturn sideways and stand up straight. The Left and Right-Somersault Positions are the most strenuous skills in the Somersault Turning. Arrow-Set Position is to lunge forward with big sudden strides and turn a somersault.

194

Back-Somersault Position is that the body somersaults backward. The back must first slightly incline to the right. In the case of stretching out the left hand to let it fall on the ground with the body slightly inclining to the left and tumbling on the left hand, thus proping up on one hand with the help of force. This is commonly called "Overturning Wagon On the Flat Ground". Thrusting-Tumbling Position is that the body crouches down and somersaults backward. Before touching the ground, sustain the body with one hand. As soon as the body touches the ground, the body rolls on this hand and then prop oneself up with this hand, Both hands can be put into use alternatively. This is commonly called "Carp's Leaping" (the carp strengthens itself). Upward-Tumbling Position is to tumble backward on the back. While tumbling, the head must bend forward a little and must not touch the ground. At the same time, use the left hand or the right hand to touch the ground. As soon as the body touches the ground it rolls on the hand which will support the body to stand up. This is called "Iron-Board Bridge". Bending Over Somersault Position is to stand with two legs together and then tumble forward. While tumbling, the body must be erect and the knees must not be bent. Before touching the ground, bend arms and clench fists and make the fists and forearms touch the ground and prop oneself up on both hands. This is commonly called "Tiger-Pouncing Gesture". As to the Rolling Position, it is rather difficult to do. It requires the process of crooking the waist and embracing the elbows. And make use of the force of both arms to sustain the shoulders above the ground and at the same time make use of the force of both legs to make the body horizontally lie on the ground and roll forward. At the start, one might make slow progress and feel painful. From day to day, he can do eighteen rollings within a short time

(Fig. 55).

Fig. 55

Brief Introduction

1. Somersault Turning is one of the hard and externalstrong arts in the seventy-two consummate skills of internal and external Gongfu which the Shaolin Temple has inherited secretly. It belongs to the Gong of both Yang Gang character and internal strong Qi. This is a specific exercise of the body's tumbling.

2. The person's internal organs are hung up inside the chest and abdomen. While being shaken, their positions usually move with the result

196

that he may feel painful and stifling and even suffer from internal hemorrhage. Shaolin Wushu is a sort of violent and antagonistic sport. In the actual combat, one may be injured by the faulty or careless falling movement. Some boxers are frightened by the shock resulted from the practice of falling. Thus, it is practically significant that this exercise of Somersault Turning is worth doing. Through the exercise, the trainee can play a positive role in acquiring harmony, speed, strength and quickness. The broad masses of trainees are fond of practising this skill.

3. "Somersault Turning" requires much effort for one to practise in the Shaolin Wushu Exercise. Its characteristics are those of requesting the trainees to make a landing on the ground with some parts of his body lying flat. Therefore, one needs strength, speed, nimbleness and harmony. It is better to do a good preparation before somersault. While training one must make reasonable use of the techniques, otherwise he may be hurt or get internal injury. So, before training, one should do the usual preparation so as to limber up his joints. While training, as soon as the body touches the ground, one should tuck up his body to produce a cushioning effect at the same moment. While tucking up, one's action must be harmonious and smooth. While making somersault, one is to touch a possibly wider space of the ground and prevent him from suffering injuries. For instance, in the exercise of Forward Falling With Elbow Bent (Zeibei), it may produce a cushioning effect to make the forearm and palms flatly touch the ground. On the contrary, his wrist may be injured if he sustains the ground with palms only. In addition, before the moment of somersaulting, try to close Qi and gather Qi so as to make the various parts of the body co-ordinate systematically. Be alert to prevent the brain and inner organs from injuring.

4. Key to the Exercise : the Shaolin Master says that it is rather difficult for one to acquire this skill. One may feel painful at the start. His internal organs can be injured too. Don't make haste. "Somersault Turning" is commonly called "Eighteen Rollings On the Ground" or "Ground-Boxing Gongfu" and is similar to Forward Somersault Position performed by itinerant entertainers. But this Arts is divided into the front and the back, left and right, including Arrow-Set, Back-Tumbling, Thrusting-Tumbling, Upward-Tumbling and Bending-Over Tumbling, etc. Somersault Turning is ranked as an excellent skill throughout the ages for its Sixty-Four Sets. It requires much effort for us to master this Arts.

FIFTY-SIXTH

Anti-Broadsword &. Anti-Spear Arts

First, begin with the practice of various Soft-Bones Gongfu, i. e. Soft-Legs, Soft-Waist, etc. Then, continue to acquire the Eye-Technique. It is a fundamental skill for the boxer to practise the three positions of Body, Hands and Eyes. In the actual combat, one has to depend on the vision of his eyes, otherwise, it would not be possible for one to deal with it. At the beginning, one must concentrate his attention on his position illustrated in Arhat Arts. After having accomplished the art of concentration, turn to count the number of things. First count the number of stable things. At leisure, count the number of bricks in the house, or the number of tiles on the opposite house. Further more, attempt to count or estimate how many tiles there are in a row. It is not easy to do. Then, pile the tiles high up for about one metre. And, estimate and tell the number of tiles at once. After this course of counting the stable things, try to estimate the number of living things. For instance, estimate and tell how many ducks there are in the pool. It is rather burdensome for one to tell the number of moving ducks. Practice makes perfect. One

199

should be wholly absorbed and in half a year he can get the preliminary result. Then, make every effort to estimate the number of smaller things, for example, the sparrows, dragon flies, mosquitoes and ants. Had one made successes in estimating and telling the number of thousands of ants in the distance of five steps away, he could be considered to have reached the climax. Apart from the skill of the vision of eyes, one should attempt to practise the skills of step position and the body plus step position. They are very effective for practising the arts of Three Cai Stakes, Seven-Star Stakes, Nine-Star Stakes and Plum-Blossom Stakes, etc. It is rather difficult to learn the Body Position. First, choose a square, bury the bamboo-poles or stakes of different sizes and different lengths irregularly into the ground and spread the lime between them. The distance between the stakes is not to be more than one foot. The learner is to walk on his side quickly among the stakes and should take care not to touch the stakes and also not to tread on the lime. While rushing, don't follow a certain way but should rush here and there, just like the butterfly flying around the flowers and the snakes wriggling in the grass. At the start, it is laborious for him to do it. But the more he walks, the quicker he rushes. Then, the trainee can fix sharp knives, hooks and thorns on the stakes and spread the iron-puncture vines on the ground. If he can go into and go out at ease, he will be taken to have reached the point of highest development (Fig. 56).

Brief Introduction

1. Anti-Broadsword &. Anti-Spear Arts, also called Entering Into Broadswords Barehanded Arts, is one of the soft and external-strong arts in the seventy-two consummate skills of internal and external Gongfu

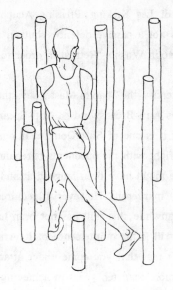

Fig. 56

which the Shaolin Temple has inherited secretly. It belongs to both Yin Rou Energy and Yang Gang character. This is a specific exercise of dodging ability.

2. Anti-Broadsword &. Anti-Spear Arts is the skill with high degree of difficulty, high precision and high standard for the sake of dealing with the opponent's attacking in the actual combat. Outwardly, the Arts refers to dodge the opponent. Inwardly, it consumes one's energy and help one to control the commanding position while the opponent launches a violent attack. Through the practice, one can fully make use of all parts

of joints, such as one's head, shoulders, elbows, hands, thighs, knees, etc. to dodge and attack, i. e. one can adapt himself to changing conditions with the skills of Leg Kicking, Pressing Acupoints and Seizing. Therefore, the skill is not a passive defence, but an active attack. The saying goes in the Shaolin Wushu "Retreat in order to advance; Defence for attacking. "

3. Key to the Exercise: the Shaolin Master says that it is quite peculiar to call this skill as Anti-Broadsword & Anti-Spear Arts. It seems to be queer but actually it is one of Soft Gongfu. If one told an amateur boxer: "I am able to fight with the opponents barehanded and I will not be injured at all. ", he might have been laughed at and said to be a liar. But this skill is really marverous. However, it requires much effort for one to practise it. Meanwhile, this skill has not been handed down completely. The dodging skill is the quintessence of it. After having accomplished the Arts, don't fear that you come under attack from all sides. But you must spend more than ten years in achieving this Arts. Nowadays, rather few people practise this Arts.

Stone-Pillar Arts

First, one must devote a lot of time and energy in the riding-horse stance. At least do it for about dozens of frequency each day. Step by step, increase the times and decrease the frequency. Afterwards, go to practise the skill of standing on the stakes after he can stand in riding-horse stance on the ground for two hours without feeling gasping or sweating. Now, two pieces of stakes are buried into the ground, two feet in height. The distance between them is just as wide as that of riding-horse stance. The learner is to stand on riding-horse stance on the stakes and it is laborious for him to apply force. So at the start, his feet will not be sturdy and his body may sway to all sides. After three months' exercise, he can get rid of his pain and stand for a longer time. Meanwhile, the learner must direct his Qi to flow to Dantian. Besides he must direct Qi to flow downward to make the body stronger and tougher. Later place a stone slab on his legs. The stone slab is rectangular with an ear on both sides. A stone slab of 20 – 30 catties is to begin with. After practising for three months, add 10 catties of weight of stone slabs in succession.

203

Satisfatory effects will result only when one can bear the stone slabs of 100 catties in weight on the legs and stand in riding-horse stance on the stakes for about one hour without feeling gasping or sweating(Fig. 57).

Fig. 57

Brief Introduction

1. Stone-Pillar is one of the hard and internal-strong arts in the seventy-two consummate skills of internal and external Gongfu which the Shaolin Temple has inherited secretly. It belongs to that of Yang Gang character. This is a specific exercise of the legs. It is also called "Riding-Horse Stance Arts. "

2. The common saying goes in the Shaolin Wushu: "Before fighting, first practise the Arts of standing on stakes. " "Stake" refers to the wood log or stone pillar buried erect into the ground with one end. The stake arts in the Shaolin Wushu means that the "Stake" stands quite stable, steady and firm. It can be divided into three types. The first is that of a standing stake, f. i. "Stone Pillar". It trains the strength of the lower part body; the second, "Beating Stakes", f. i. "Meteor Stake". It is to train the strength of all parts of the body; the third, "Walking Stake", f. i. "Plum-Blossom Stakes". It needs agility of the whole body.

3. The Boxing Guide says: To practise the riding-horse stance is not to improve the strength of the legs only, but also makes the Qi and Blood flow down and strengthen the muscles and bones. Therefore, no matter where you stand, you can not be pushed away, even though you stay on the narrow and dangerous spot. As stated by "Secret Of Shaolin Boxing", among the footworks, the riding-horse stance is taken as the first requirement. (which is also called "Standing Stakes"). The second is that of shrinking and stretching the body so that your kidney will be strengthened and you can be quick in your movement and can prevent you from suffering back aching and legs aching. The satisfatory effects will result only when the learner can stand on the narrow and dangerous spot with his back and front soles of his feet and can not be pushed or dragged away. The above-mentioned method refers to the exercise of the legs. The tree without roots can be easily pushed away. Therefore, the riding-horse stance is the basic arts and is the first step for one to acquire Wushu. After having mastered the riding-horse stance skillfully, one's Qi can flow to Dantian and he is just like a "Roly-Poly" which never falls down to the ground. Afterwards, one can practise all sorts of skills days

after days. At the beginning, the weaker man may feel painful and ache all over. On the contrary, he will feel that his power before training is much stronger than that of after training. This is called "Transforming Force". But till now, don't fear any difficulty but continue to advance. For instance, in the first day, one can stand in riding-horse stance for about two hours and in the second day, he must increase the training time. While getting tired, just take a rest. One will get initial result only when he can stand pain with his Qi flowing to Dantian. After one's legs become stronger, turn to practise the skill of hands. (Details to follow).

4. "Stone-Pillar Arts" (i. e. Riding-Horse Stance Arts And Stakes Arts), is noted for its firmness, sturdiness and offensiveness in the Shaolin Wushu. Meanwhile, it is also a fundamental skill to improve the strength of legs. "Stake Force" embodies the force of pliability, neither complete Gang (Hardness) nor entire Rou (Softness). It exerts force invisibly, but the force is strong enough to break anything. So while standing in riding-horse stance, one should apply the power skillfully. It is seen to be slow, but it is actually speedy. And one can get twice the result with half the effort. So the poem says: "Moveless stake skill has invisible strength and in the quiteness, mighty force can be applied." Thereby, the Shaolin monks lay great emphasis on "Stone Pillar Exercise". Nowadays, there still exist forty-eight sinking pits in four rows on the aquare brick ground in the Thousand Buddhists Palace, Shaolin Temple, Song Mount. Henan Province. It is said that they were the historical remains which were left by the Shaolin monks who used to stand there on riding-horse stance to exert their force.

5. As the Boxing Proverb says: Unsteady steps make irregular fists; Slow steps make clumsy fists. "The traditional Eight-Position in the

Shaolin Wushu requires "Sticky Steps" (Bu-Sai Nian) i. e. the steps must be nimble and sturdy. "Step Technique" in the Shaolin Wushu is held responsible for "Steadiness" and "Fastness". Therefore, the steps must be quick in the movement and firm as if the legs are sticking on the ground. Although the steady condition of the upper limbs and body is very important, yet emphasis should be paid on the strength of the leg, for the legs are the supporting points of the body in the actual combat. If one's legs are unsteady, he can not control his centre of gravity, nor can he master the function of inertia. In that case, he may fall on the ground without being beaten. Therefore, no matter how he leaps and pounces, his lower part of the body must be as stable as Mount. Taishan. And it is most effective for the trainees to practise the "Stone-Pillar Arts". Through the practice of this Arts, one improves not only the strength of legs, but also the ability of springing and grasping. The Shaolin Wushu requires the ability of "Acting Like Great Waves" (In the movement, one's action is to be like the surging waves" or ten thousand horses galloping); "Calmness Like Mount" (While calming down, one's gesture must be as solemn as Mount. Taishan); Standing Like Pine (The feet on the ground are like the tall and straight pines. Its calmness hides its movement inside, i. e. calmness combines with movement.); Heavier Like Iron (just like the iron falling down), etc. "All these standard patterns should be acquired through the practice of "Stone-Pillar". Thereby, this skill plays a determining role in the Shaolin Wushu.

6. Key to the Exercise: the Shaolin Master says that this Arts is one of the main positions in the Stake Arts, and it is a secret skill of legs training. After having accomplished this Arts, one can act like a pillar standing, even if he is pushed by a strong person. The feet's power is re-

ally indispensable to the boxers. Forceless legs make steps unsteady. The unsteady steps make one defeated. When successful, one's power of legs will seem to be as heavy as a thousand catties in weight. He will appear like the bastion of iron. One must at least spend more than five years in practising the skill and he should practise it assiduously and diligently.

FIFTY-EIGHTH

Plum-Blossom Stakes Arts

First, it is not necessary to stand on the stakes. Paint some plum-blossoms on the ground with lime. The distance between two blossoms is to be about two or three feet. Every blossom has five circles looked like the petals. Each petal is taken to be a stake. The distance between two petals is about one foot and the diameter of each circle is about three inches. After painting the blossoms, the trainee appoints one of the petals in each plumblossom to be a false stake and bears it in mind. He is to stand on the "nominal" stake of the middle plum-blossom. While standing, the trainee just uses a foot and applies force to his toes so as to stand on his toes. The trainee can plan the leaping procedure in his mind, for instance, the left three, the right four; the front two, the back five. Do it just according to the existing condition. It is better to ask a person to make shoutings. He leaps on the nominal stakes according to that person's shouting. If a shouting "right second blossom, first stake" is given he is to jump immediately to a "stake" on the right side of the second blossom. The rest may be done similarly. But he must avoid jumping to the false stake in each blossom. While jumping, his toes should step on the centre of the circle. When he begins to jump on the nominal stakes, he should never incline to one side, or he will be defeated. And at the beginning, he is unable to step on the centre of the nominal stake, so it is better for him to practise the art of jumping to and fro on the four nominal stakes of the same blossom. Then, turn to practise this Arts on the eight nominal stakes of two blossoms. Step by step, increase the number of blossoms. He can not go to practise the skill on the real stakes until he is a hundred percent sure that he has completely mastered the skill of stepping in the above mentioned ways on the ground. The real stake is made of wood pole, 3. 5 feet in length, two inches in diametre, and broad in the upper part but slim in the lower part. Bury them into the ground where the plum-blossoms have been painted. And on the false stakes' spots, the stakes should be buried into the ground about one or two inches deep. And the earth on this part of the ground must be loose, so that, when he accidently falls down, he will not be seriously injured. After all the stakes should have been buried in the centre of the petals. The learner goes on to practise this skill according to the previously mentioned method. When he can jump on the stakes at ease, he may gradually increase the height of the stakes and place some iron puncture vine around the stakes. When the height of the stakes is increased to three feet high, he can be said to have made a sure success. Go on training. It is better to carry with him a bag of cinnabar. Before the cinnabar is put into use, it must be fired and put into the pig blood to let it soaked, otherwise he will be hurt. He can also use the copper rings instead of the cinnabar. He should have to spend three years to reach a summit skill of this Arts (Fig. 58).

210

Brief Introduction

1. Plum-Blossom Stakes Arts is one of the soft and internal-strong arts in the seventy-two consummate skills of internal and external Gongfu which the Shaolin Temple has inherited secretly. This is a specific exercise of the footworks. It is one of the traditional Stakes Arts.

2. "Seven-Blossom Stakes Arts" was developed from the ancient "Seven Pan-Drums Arts". In the dynasties of Han and Wei or Jin "Seven Pan-Drums Arts" had been a kind

Fig. 58

of fashionable artistry whereby the actors danced on the seven drums to the sound music. After Tang Dynasty, because of the improvement of techniques, it was developed from "Drums" to "Stakes". In addition to the Plum-Blossom Stakes Arts in the Shaolin Wushu, (the stakes are arranged in the East, South, West and North and the centre with the form just like a Plum-Blossom), there are still Seven-Stars Stakes Arts (its arrangment is just like that of the Big Dipper), Nine-Stars Stakes Arts (its arrangment is to bury a group of three stakes each in the front, middle and back, making nine stakes in all to form a square). Big-Dipper Stakes

211

Arts (its arrangment is divided into twelve rows from left to right. In each row, bury three stakes in the front, middle and back respectively, i. e. thirty-six stakes in all, with the meaning to represent thirty-six Big Dippers) etc.

3. Through the practice of "Plum-Blossom Stakes Arts", one improves not only the power of the lower part of his body, but also the agility of his body. It is a fundamental skill of Shaolin Wushu. But it differs from the other Stakes Arts, for the area of Plum-Blossom Stakes Arts is smaller than that of the others. The man who stands on the stake should step on it with the front sole. If he is not careful, he may fall down. Meanwhile, there is a certain space between the stakes and each action asks for accuracy, otherwise, he will slip and fall on the ground and be injured by the other stake. Beacuae of its high degree of difficulty and danger, this Arts is highly technical.

4. Key to the Exercise: the Shaolin Master says that the stake Gong-fu is an exercise of the body's agility and footworks. It lays emphasis on the jumping skill. When successful, if you happen to meet your opponent, you will be able to face danger fearlessly. Apart from the jumping skill, one should lay stress on his eye-sight. Having achieved the Arts, one will be quick and nimble in the movement and can defeat the opponent at ease. As for the Arts of Three-Cai Stakes, Seven-Stars Stakes, Nine-Stars Dodging Stakes and Dodging Bricks, etc. the training method is similar to that of the Plum-Blossom Arts.

212

Meteor Stakes Arts

It is also done with ease. Bury a large bamboo-pole into the ground as a stake, bind it with ropes outside. Now, stand in front of the stake, bump against it with your head, palms, shoulders, elbows, wrists, arms, legs, and buttocks, or beat, pat and kick it, and so on. And in the course of bumping and beating, he must presume himself that he is beating at a certain part of the opponent's body. At the start, one may get painful, but as time goes on, his muscle will be strengthened, and his internal power will be improved. The colour of one's body will appear to be iron-like,. Now the trainee is invincible in the actual combat(Fig. 59).

Brief Introduction

1. Meteor Stake Arts is one of the hard and external-strong arts in the seventy-two consummate skills of internal and external Gongfu which the Shaolin Temple has inherited secretly. It belongs to that of Yang Gang character. This is a specific exercise of the various parts of the body. It is one of the traditional stake exercises.

213

Fig. 59

2. "Meteor Stake Arts" is also called "Stake Target Arts". The method of training power differs from that of "Sand-Bag Arts". It is also called "Fixed Stake Arts", "Dead Stake Arts". Through the practice of "Meteor Stake Arts", one can improve and strengthen the muscle's acting force and reacting force on the part of limbs. Not only does it suit the needs of judging the real circumstance and the distance in the actual combat, but also it acquires the skills of taking an offensive. One can achieve marvellous results in the case of taking an offensive by combining the power of "Ten Fists" of Shaolin Wushu into "a Single Fist" with

214

irresistible force. (Note: "Ten Fists" refers to mean that there lie ten parts of body all of which have power and the combined power is concentrated in a single fist which will be able to vanquish the enemy. The "Ten Fists" consists of the head, shoulders, elbows, palms, fists, fingers, buttocks, groin, knees and feet.)

3. "Meteor Stake Arts" is particular about its moving in harmony and its softness dwelles in hardness. It "upholds vigorous energy, not mere force "in the actual combat. The boxer is required to be speedy, accurate and powerful. Of course, one will naturally improve his force after a long-run exercise. In short, don't make haste. Proceed in an orderly way steap by step.

4. Key to the Exercise: the Shaolin Master says that one may reach the crowning point after three years' training. The majority of the people in the five provinces in northeastern China are fond of practising this skill, too.

Leaping & Jumping Arts

The training method is not beyond the scope of binding the legs with lead slabs, but the lead slabs must be treated by a special process, otherwise, one might be hurt. First, the lead slab must be fired reddened. Put it into the pig blood, let it soak the blood for one day. Again take it out and then fire it and let it soak the blood for seven times. When the blood permeats the lead, the colour of the lead will become green purple to become "Dead Lead". Then the lead should be buried into the earth for forty-nine days and its poison can be eliminated. Then, clean it with water. Now the treated lead slabs can be utilized. Wrap each lead slab with a cloth bag and bind them to the legs, the shoulders and the backs, from light to heavy, up to 18 catties in weight. First, practise to run up the hills every day. That is the foundation of the skill. After one year, continue to practise running on the brink of a vat, i. e. walking along the edge of a vat. The next step is to strive to practise running on the standing bricks, i. e. to put the usual long bricks to stand erect on the ground. The learner runs on them freely and they will not tumble over. Now he

216

has reaped the first fruit. Then stretch his knees and waist straight with the help of the supporting force of his legs and palms and make every effort to jump up and leap up. If he can jump high up to one foot he may release the lead bags, and with his waist and knees bending, try his best to jump up. He will find himself to be able to jump to a height of over 6. 6 metres. He has not come to preliminary success. Only when his both legs can stamp hard on the ground with the help of the elasticity of his knees, can he leap high in the air. It is to this extent that he can be said to have reached the zenith (Fig. 60).

Brief Introduction

1. Leaping & Jumping Arts is one of the soft and internal-strong arts in the sevvnty-two consummate skills of internal and external Gongfu which the Shaolin Temple has inherited secretly. It belongs to that of Yang Gang character. This is a specific exercise of the body's leaping ability. It is one of the traditional Light-Body Skills.

2. Leaping & Jumping Arts is one of the Light-Body Skills. Light-Body Skill (Qing Gong) has a long history. According to historical records, in the third year of Wei Dynasty (527. A. D.) Emperor Liang-Wu ordered somebody to invite Master Da-Mo to visit Nanjin (Jin Ling). When they talked, they could not agree with each other. They broke up in discord. Hence, Master Da-Mo picked up a piece of reed and put it on the water. He stood on it drifting across the Yangtze River. (Nowadays it is still widely known that Master Da-Mo drifted across the Yangtze River with a piece of reed only)At present, there still stands a tablet of "Across the Yangtze River with a Single Reed" at the back of Heaven-Empire Palace of Shaolin Temple in Song Mount. of Henan

Fig. 60

Province. It was built in the eleventh year of Emperor Yuan Da Deh of
Yuan Dynasty (1307 A. D.). It is a rare work of art. This is one of the
earliest legends about the arts of Light Body in the Shaolin Wushu. In the
past ages, many Shaolin monks were versed in Light-Body Arts, f. i.
Master Zhi-Yuan, Master Ji-Qing, Master Yi-Guan, Master Zhen-Jun,
etc. They were all representive figures. In the modern history, those who
were skilled in Light-Body Arts were Li Jing-Hua, Du Xing-Wu, Liu

218

Shen-Yan, and so on. Li Jing-Hua, whose nickname was "Swallow Li-Shan", was famous for his being a chivarous robber. Besides that, the son of "Jin-Door Chivarous Man" named Dong Ge was expert in this skill. He once made a public performance of Light-Body Arts in Guan Dong Martial Hall in Tianjin. He tied an apple with a piece of cotton string and hung it more than one metre high above his head. Dong-Ge and his disciple stood under the apple. Both of them simultanously leaped up to bite the apple oppositely. Their actions were made in harmony. While they were biting the apple oppositely, the apple did not move at all. When leaping and jumping, their bodies seemed as light as those of swallows. And no sound was heard. The poem says: "Shaolin Light-Gongfu is the most excellent in Arts. Only the trainee who are assidious and diligent can acquire the skill. His movement follows his Qi and his head is regarded as the headquarters. Only when his mind directs Dantian, can he burst out strong tiger-pouncing power. Even if his feet are bound with iron-tiles, he can still leap over the sand-pit. He may be seen dressed with beautiful arms rings and copper-keys. At one shouting, he can leap up to four feet high as if he has got rid of everything to fly into the air. "

3. The traditional "Twelve Patterns" in the Shaolin Wushu requires the learner to jump like an ape (the gesture and movement of jumping must be quick and nimble like an ape), to fall on the ground like a magpie (the gesture of falling must be light and steady, just like a magpie.) and to be as light as a leaf (the posture of his body should be as light as a leaf.). In order to reach these aims, the trainee must practise the skills of Light Body, f. i. " Leaping and Jumping Arts" etc. Through the practice for dozens of years, the hidden energy inside his body will be brought into full play.

4. Key to the Exercise: the Shaolin Master says that the "Energy Road" of his skill belongs to that of Softness. Many boxers in the past practised this Arts.

Jumping &. Leaping Arts

At the beginning of training, the trainee binds his body fast with a load of a small quantity of iron sand. Dig a pit, one foot deep and capable of holding two persons in circumference. Stand inside it and jump up and down freely. Then, jump out of and into the pit as many successive times as he can at different intervals in a day. At the start he may feel it rather easy to jump out with only an easy motion of his feet without bending an effort to make a soar, for the pit is shallow and the weight of the sand iron is light. By and by, for an interval of every ten days or every half a month the pit is to be dug an inch deeper and the weight of one tael of iron sand is to be added at the same time. Thus, the deeper the pit is dug, the heavier will the weight be added to his body and the harder will he find to make a jump. When the pit is dug to a depth of 3 feet, the period of training should be longer. With the lapse of time the pit measures 5 to 7 feet deep and then 7 to 10 feet deep and correspondently the weight of iron sand bound to his body will measure about 5 to 7 catties. Only at this time when he is still able to jump out of and jump into the pit of

221

such a depth with the carriage of such a heavy load of iron sand, can he be considered to have made a big accomplishment. With the removal of iron sand he will naturally be able to skip over a wall even if it is 20 feet high without making gestures to gather his strength. He cannot reach such a summit level unless he has spent more than 3 to 5 years of training in this way (Fig. 61).

Fig. 61

Brief Introduction

1. Jumping Arts, also called "Surmounting Distance Skill", is one of the soft and internal-strong arts in the seventy-two consummate skills of internal and external Gongfu which the Shaolin Temple has inherited secretly. This is a specific exercise of one's jumping ability. It is one of the traditional Light-Body Arts.

2. "Jumping And Leaping Arts", expounded in "Secret of Shaolin Boxing Arts" : "It is definitely not easy to practise jumping with his body erect. For an early youth in his teens it is possible for him to soar up to a height of over 20 feet high, if he devotes himself to make practice for 3 years. Should he keep on practising without interruption, by and by, he can still reach an increasingly high level. " During the reigns of Dao Guan and Xian Fen in the Qing Dynasty, Northerners were talented in this realm of art and skill. Recently, people in Dian (Yunnan province) and Qian (Gui-Zhou Province) have a great fondness of practising this skill. As far as we know, there are more than 12 people in Dian and Qian, who have won their fame for their skill. Their training process is as follows. At the start, dig a pit, about five inches in depth with its width large enough to hold two feet. While training, the learner stands inside, stretches his waist and legs and jumps up and down for not more than thirty or fifty times each time. Later on he increases the number of times day after day. Take a rest when he feels tired. Avoid being exhausted. The beginner at least should spend half a year before being able to jump out of the pit of 5 inches in depth, because he has to make use of his strength with his waist and legs stretched. However, should he then make gestures by bending his waist, he will be able to make a soaring jump to a height of over 10 feet. It is the result of 2 or 3 years of strenuous training

and is by no means a make-haste task. After that, he is to bind some shaped slabs of lead to the skin bones of the legs, each slab of lead being about five or ten catties in weight. The slabs are to be added by degrees to match his acquired strength and the level of his practising skill. If he is able to jump out of a pit of over 1 foot deep under a load of lead slabs of 20 to 30 catties in weight bound on his right and left legs, he will then be capable of making a soaring jump to a height of tens of feet after the removal of dead slabs. It is sure for him to make successes if he pays painstaking efforts to make practices.

3. Key to the Exercise: On this Arts, as said by the Shaolin master boxers, it belongs to one kind of Body-Light Arts and is an important Arts indispensable to those who practise martial arts. It is necessary to make double efforts in the course of making practice. In the case of normal leaping and jumping arts it is not at all surprising if he at a distance of 5 feet away makes gestures to pluck up his courage before jumping. Only when he can skip over a high wall or a steep barrier from the spot where he stands, can he be competent to acquire this skill.

Flying Arts

The beginner binds both his legs with gunny bags filled full with lead or iron sands. At times, keep on running in the open air every day until being exhausted. At the start, the weight of lead or iron sands must not be too heavy. Later on every few days, each bag can be added with one tael of lead. The more he makes practices, the more lead will be added in till the total weight of the lead will be about four or five catties. At first, he may feel painful, but day after day, he will not be feeling uneasy. Several years after, he will not feel uneasy if he removes the bags away. But he is not able to achieve this Arts until he walks rapidly on the places full of bumps and holes posturing nimbly like an ape (Fig. 62).

Brief Introduction

1. Flying Arts, also called Night-Walking Skill, Land-Flying Skill, or Long-Distance Walking Alone Skill, is one of the soft and internal-strong arts in the seventy-two consummate skills of internal and external

Fig. 62

Gongfu which the Shaolin Temple has secretly inherited. This is a specific exercise of one's running and walking ability. It is one of the traditional Light-Body Arts.

2. Legend has it that Yang Da-Yan in the Wei Dynasty was versed in this Arts. When starting to launch South expedition, Emperor Li-Kun selected martial boxers. Da-Yan wanted to join the army. Li-Kun saw him appearing queer and refused to enlist him. Da-Yan laughed and said: "Your Majesty, don't you think that I am too young to join the army? Please let me show my skill." With these words, he took a rope, 9.9 metres in length, tied it to his hair and rushed forward. There and then the

226

rope was stretched straight like an arrow. Even if a fighter rode a horse to run after him, he could not catch up with him. The people all around there were astonished at watching this "Land-Flying Skill". Li-Kun was completely convinced. A song born of this legend says to the effect that " : If a learner makes practice with a load of 1000 cattiesbound on his legs daily, he will turn all of a sudden to be fleetfooted runner. Hence the "Rope Star" will thereby naturally be able to leap swiftly on the ravine and creep along the steep precipice looking like a swimming string. He who wants to know the secret therein is to bind his legs with irontiles for tens of years. "

3. Key to the Exercise; the Shaolin Master Boxer says that it is one of the Light-Body Arts. And it is an exercise of walking skill. The method of eyes training has been explained in detail in the Arhat Arts. - The learner should make up his mind and stick to his training. It is better to make slow progress than fast one. When successful, he can combine this art with Jumping and Leaping Arts with stretched feet. Thus, no wonder that he will be able to acquire the consummate skill of leaping onto roofs and vaulting over walls.

Light-Body Arts

First, set seven large stone vats full of water, and walk on the edge of vats, i. e. Running Vats Edge. To begin with carrying on his back a gunny bag filled with a few catties of iron sands or lead which should be soaked in the pig—blood. Half a month later, take a gourd ladle of water out of the vat, and add a few taels of iron sand. After having finished a months' training, take some water away and add some iron sand again. - Then, repeatedly make practice as above said until the vat is empty and the weight of the iron sand is 5 catties. Finally, the trainee is to walk on the edge of the empty vat. Then, use a bamboo basket, filled with the iron-sand, to take the place of a vat. Make every endeavour to practise the skill of walking on the brink of the basket. Achievements can be made only when he can walk on the edge of an empty basket. Again, spread some fine sand on the road, 1 foot in thickness. Cover the surface of the sand with thin mulberry leaves. Walk on the surface. There will clearly be footprints on it. After a long-range exercise, there will not remain any footprints on the sand. Then he has reached the point of highest

228

achievement (Fig. 63)

Brief Introduction

    1. Light-Body Arts is one of
the soft and internal-strong arts
in the seventy-two consummate
skills of internal and external
Gongfu which the Shaolin Temple has inherited secretly. This is
a specific exercise of the body's
ability. It is one of the traditional
Light Body Skills.

    2. As recorded in "Secret of
Shaolin Boxing" ··· the people in
Chuan (Sichuan Province), Er
(Hubei Province) saw that Teng
(Teng Hai-Zi, a Shaolin Boxing
Master) had few compan-
ions. The Chuan and Er people
wanted to beat Teng with
sticks. Teng leaped up at once and

Fig. 63

dozens of them were at once thrown by him into the river. The rest covered their heads with their hands and sneaked away like rats. On the second day, thousands of people in Chuan and Er came back again. Teng
leaped up and thrusted out his fists. The Chuan and Er people around him
were casted away. While fighting, Teng looked like an angry hawk flying
and preying across the sky. He was dexterous and nimble in his motion,

229

his actions being like a flash of lightning. " "Diary of A Qing Officer" records to the similar effect: "There was a man, his surname being Zheng, in the West Countryside. He had an enormous appetite. Every day, he touched his abdomen and asked himself:" So large a stomach. What is the use of it? "He was famed for his big abdomen. He was strong and versed in boxing. He crossed the river like a dragonfly skimming the surface of the water. He could leap high up to many meters, overlooking the city-wall. ".

3. Key to the Exercise: the Shaolin Boxer Master says that it is most arduous for a learner to practise the Light-Body Arts. As the body is more than a hundred catties in weight, to fly like a butterfly or a swallow would have been considered to be impossible. However, the training method is similar to Leaping and Jumping Arts, Flying Arts and Single-Rope Penetrating Arts. When successful, he will not leave behind any footprint on the snow or grass while flying and leaping. This Arts, another name is "Tread on Duckweed across the Water and Leaving behind No Footprints on Snow". The learner should spend 12 years in practising to complete this Arts.

Single-Rope Penetrating Arts

The training process can be divided into several stages. At the beginning, it is similar to that of Flying Arts and Light-Body Arts. Firstly, the learner carries a load of lead and runs rapidly on the flat ground and then practises jumping and leaping on the hill-road. Afterwards he is to make practice by putting stone slabs in a bamboo basket and walking on its brink. d by, take the stone slabs out of the basket and step on its brink. How to proceed to make practice in this respect has been illustrated before. But, please remember that the lead should be soaked in the pig-blood and become ''dead lead'' to avoid the legs being hurt. Secondly, the learner takes a thin and long wood pole, fastens its both ends to two opposite sides and hangs the pole to a height of two or three feet. Then he makes every effort to run on it. At the start, the wood pole may swing all the time. Only when he runs on it and it does not move at all, will he be said to have accomplished this Arts. Thirdly, he is to use a rope to take the good place of the wood pole and fasten the rope to two bamboo stands. As the rope is very soft, it will sink down and sway to and fro while

231

the learner runs on it. So it's more difficult for a learner to make training. He will accomplish this Arts when he walks on a rope which doesn't
sway at all. Lastly, if a learner fastens a rope to either side of the river
banks and walk or run on it across the river, he can be taken to have
made accomplishment (Fig. 64).

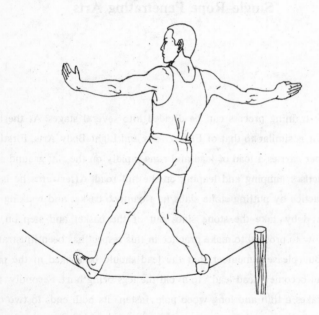

Fig. 64

Brief Introduction

1. Single-Rope Penetrating Arts is also called Monk Da-Mo Cross-

232

ing River or Flying Over the Water. The common saying runs : Treading On Soft Rope Arts is one of the soft and internal-strong arts in seventy-two consummate skills of internal and external Gongfu which the Shaolin Temple has inherited secretly.

2. Key to the Exercise : the Shaolin Master says that it is the skill of "Treading on Duckweed across the Water and Leaving No Footprint on Snow". Though it's really laborious to master the Arts, he should make great efforts to practise it. When successful, he can skim over the surface of the water with the help of a pliable substance, such as bamboo sheets, reed, etc. In the past, the legend has it : "Master Monk Da-Mo went to the West alone. He used only a piece of reed to help him cross the river. "His skill is the outcome of this sort of Gongfu, too. In short, one should spend more than ten years to acquire this Arts and must pass through a course of training painstakingly and modestly. The liquid medicine used to wash the feet should compose of a kind of Chinese traditional medicine called Di-Gu-Pi, and salt and so on so that his blood and his energy of life can be harmonious and his skin relaxed.

Penetration Arts

First, practise the Arts of Leaping-Up Platform by leaping from up to down on a platform like a square table of 6. 6 meters in four dimensions. Stand on the platform at attention. Sink down his body. Raise his hands at the same time followed by raising his body. Apply strength to his feet and leap forward with his two arms stretched straight. The whole body must be postured in a straight line. In front of the platform, there lies a exceedingly long and large sand pit, in which the sand is three feet in thickness and each of the four angles of which stands a firmly driven-in stake. Then, fasten a large rope woven net to the stakes at a height of 2 feet above the sand surface. The trainer can safely jump down from the platform without being hurt. After completing the platform leaping Arts with success, then turn to practise the Arts of "Leaping Over the Bar". Between two wood poles installed on both sides of the sand pit is fixed with a horizontal bar at a height of three feet above the sand surface. Stand 20 feet away from the bar. Direct his Qi and rush forward toward the bar. On approaching near the bar, apply strength to touch the

234

ground and leap over the bar. Just like the "High Jump", he must keep his body in a straight line to leap in a slant position over the bar. After being versed in the skill of leaping over the bar, he is to practise leaping over a wood board of about 1.5 feet in width. The width of the wood board may vary from 1.5 feet to 3 feet. It is more strenous for him or anyone to leap over the board of 3 feet in width. Finally, place a square wood framework on the board. Practise to leap through the framework in the same manner. The number of frameworks is then to be increased from one to six or seven in a row. After his being able to leap penetrating through the row of wood frame works, he is taken to be on the approach to a much higher skill level. At last, fix sharp knives around the inside surface within the frameworks leaving a room spacious enough for the penetrating of a body. If he succeeds in penetrating the frameworks with knives fixed there in, he is taken to have attained the summit of the Arts in this respect (Fig. 65).

Brief Introduction

1. Penetration Arts is one of the soft and internal-strong arts in the seventy-two consummate skills of internal and external Gongfu which the Shaolin Temple has inherited. This is a type of specific exercise of one's leaping upward and leaping forward ability and is also a type of the traditional Light -Body Arts.

2. As recorded in the "A Sketch on Insects Chirping", a scholar wanted to revenge an insult. He learned the boxing Arts from a monk in the Shaolin Temple. The monk saw that he was very weak and asked him to face a wall of an empty room. On the wall were paintings about the boxing routines. He was ordered by the monk to make practice according

235

Fig. 65

to the routine procedure. As times went on, he got versed in them. Then he was led to a wall, in which there was a round hole and he was asked to leap to and fro through the hole. As times went on, he get quick in his movement. Once the monk saw that he was able to leap into and out of the hole and said; "Tomorrow you must be careful. " On the next day, when he leaped through the hole of the wall, he immadiately saw an iron-fork stuck in the ground in front of him. From then on, he began to make practice on weapons.

3. Key to the Exercise; Shaolin Boxer Master says that it is one of

236

the Light-Body Arts and so named because the leaping is in a slanting position. Frequently, we can often see that an acrobat plays the so-called "Leaping Through Knives-Door" and "Leaping Through Flame-Door" and so on, which belong to this sort of Gongfu. The on-lookers may feel that the player requires no effort to make the performance, but they do not know where the difficulty lies. When successful, he can leap through the hole to and fro at ease. But he should spend more than five years to practise this Arts.

Belt-Somersault Arts

At the beginning, practise the Arts of "Tiger-Leaping and Somersault" (i. e. Front Somersault) and "Leaping and Jumping" etc. Above all, this sort of free-standing exercises are requirements of a boxing learner. Then, proceed to do exercises on apparatus. Practise to do mounting and dismounting a horizontal bar. Hold the bar and mount slowly until your lower abdomen reaches the horizontal bar and dismount slowly until your feet touch the ground. Having achieved the above skill, turn to practise the "Windmill" which means grasping the bar to make your whole body circle around the horizontal bar. After having a good command of this skill, shift to the soft bar exercise. The soft bar is also called "Leather Belt Rope". Set up two 6. 6metres wood poles with a horizontal bar installed on either top of the poles. On the lower part of the bar are fixed with rings at an equal distance of 2 feet. The strong leather belts are fastened fast to the rings. The leather belts hang down to the ground. The distance between two belts is 2 feet. Stand between two leather belts. Grasp firmly two leather belts to make mounting. While applying strength to his right hand, he stretches his left hand to grasp the upper part of the adjacent belt. While exerting force to the left hand, he stretches his right hand to grasp the upper part of the adjacent belt. Similarly, while applying strength to his left hand, he stretches his left hand to grasp the upper part of the adjacent belt. After ascending to the top, he turns to dismount in the same way. On raising his body in the east side, he may swing to grasp the third rope in the west side. Thus, after grasping the third belt, he has to let go the 2nd belt in order to grasp the fourth belt in the west. After he grasps the last belt in the west, he returns to grasp the belt toward the east. Practise this Arts repeatedly till he is exhausted. It means that he has to complete the course of mounting and dismounting as well as side vaulting by means of the strong leather belts. After that, strive to practise"Back ward somersault". Hold one belt with each hand. Although it is similar to "Windmill Arts", he is to make vaulting with his arms bent backward. The trainee had better do it from quick motion to slow motion. Technically speaking, higher attainment in respect of this skill is always born of slow motion. Satisfatory effects will come if he makes landing at ease without feeling tired. After mastering" Belt-Somersault Arts, he has to go on practising" Releasing-the -Grip Leaping". Hold one leather belt with each hand. Exert great strength downward in order to raise the whole body upward. At the instant of raising up his body, he has to release the leather belts from both hands and swing forward to get hold of the upper parts of the next adjacent until he reaches the top. Then come down in the similar way. After that, begin to practise"Side Vaulting Up". It is similar to"Side Walking". For example, hold No. 1 and 2 ropes at the eastern end of the horizontal bar. Exert his strength down-ward to raise his body. Then at the instant of raising his body up, release the grip and swing westward as far as possible to catch hold of the distant two ropes , say No. 5 and 6 at the westen end. And after several months' practice to have a good command of this skill, use silk ropes of the size of a finger to replace the leather belts. Then go on practising this skill with the help of thinner and thinner silk ropes until he can also perform well by using silk ropes each of which is of the size of a finger. Practising each kind of the above mentioned arts according to the stipulated routines will lead him to have satisfactory accompliments(Fig. 66).

Fig. 66

Brief Introduction

1. Belt-Somersault Arts, also called Leather Belt Arts, is one of the soft and internal-strong arts in the seventy-two consummate skills of internal and external Gongfu which the Shaolin Temple has inherited secretly. This is a specific exercise of the body's vaulting. It is one type of the traditional Light-Body Arts.

2. Key to the Exercise: Shaolin Boxer Master says that it is one type of the Light-Body Arts. If a trainee happens to come across a steep and rugged place, he will be able to make mounting or dismounting easily with his hands resting on something even as light as the small tree leaves and branches.

Gecko-Creeping-Wall Arts

First, lie on your back, exert strong force with your elbows and heels to sustain your whole body resting against the lying place and then make a forceful treading to push the whole body to go ahead toward the head position, i. e. moving in a manner similar to Centipede-Creeping. According to the method, keep on practising the skill for about two years and you will be able to move on your back at ease like the snake creeping. Then, build a strong brick wall with some bricks projecting out to several inches and some bricks sunken into several inches. Now, press your elbows and heels on the projecting bricks with your back sticking closely on the wall. Then, move your body upward gradually. At the start, you may fail, i. e. drop down after only a slight side moving. Don't be afraid of the difficulty, Stick to make the practice of this Arts. After a long exercise for several years, you will be able to make mounting or dismounting on steep and rugged walls without difficulty. Moreover, you can also do vaulting from side to side horizontally. Later, bind your body fast with a load of some lead or sand. You can be considered to have

242

achieved a seventy percent success, if you can do vaulting up and down or side by side easily with a load of several catties of lead or sand bound on your body. Then, turn to break the projected bricks so that the wall will not be so rugged. Constant practice on this wall will make the surface of the wall to be more even. Then release the lead or sand bag from your body and continue to make the same exercise and you will feel that you are creeping like a house lizard (Fig. 67).

Brief Introduction

1. Gecko-Creeping-Wall Arts, also called "Creeping Wall Arts" or "Hanging Painting Arts", is one of the soft and internal-strong arts in the seventy-two consummate skills of internal and external Gong fu which the Shaolin Temple has inherited secretly. This is a specific exercise of the body's moving on the wall. It is one of the traditional Light-Body Skill.

2. It was recorded in "Diary from a Qing Official": " ··· A monk stepped in leisurely, rolled up his sleaves with his left hand, thrusted out his right fist. Zhen (called Zhen Big Abdomen) immediately made vaulting with his back against the wall in order to avoid the monk's Boxing. Zhen was doing "Gecko-Creeping-

Fig. 67

Wall Arts", which the Shaolin Temple inherited. The story has it that,

243

during the early years of the Republic of Cnina, a Shaolin Masterhand named Zhan Xue-Bin gave an open challenge in Da-Lu Garden in Shanghai. He crept a two-feet-wide cement board with his hands and feet like a gecko creeping. At that time, "NEWS" in Shanghai published that, when Zhen had been practising the skills, he used to jump up to a platform 6. 6 metres in height to see his master to make inquiries about Wushu. He showed clearly his supernatural skill.

3. Key to the Exercise; the Shaolin Boxer Master says that those who want to be versed in the Art of Gecko-Creeping-Wall with his back resting on the wall to do mounting and dismounting or side vaulting have to spend much time, say ten years.

SIXTY-EIGHTH

Arts of Leaping Onto Roofs And Vaulting Over Walls

The training process presents no difficulty. Before training, bind your forearms and legs with gunny-bags each of which is filled with iron sand of a smaller quantity. Every morning and evening, do" Horizontally Running" on the wall. Begin with your body lying sideways and make advance forward by moving your two feet alternatively. Keep on practising until you feel exhausted. It is necessary for you to draw yourself backward more than ten steps to gather the elastic force and then lunge sideways forward. Stamp your left foot, lunge sideways and descend with your right foot landing on the ground first to obtain at attention position. That is called" Left Form" skill. Likewise, stamp your right foot first, lunge sideways forward with your body in midair and descend with your left foot landing on the ground first to obtain at attention position. This is called" Right form" skill. After making practice of this skill for one year you can only make a first stage success of horizontally running of not more than 4 paces. The next step will be to gradually increase the weight of iron-sand day by day to a maximum weight to the

245

limit of 12 catties. The second stage success will mean that you do horizontal running of 8 paces a day. The distance of eight paces is about 5. 3 metres. Then, strive to practise running sideways with your body slanting upward. At the start, you may fall down halfway. You must not fear the difficulty met with. On the contrary, add the iron sand up to twenty catties in weight. The third stage success comes if you can run sideways upward to a distance of eight paces with a load of 20 catties of iron sand. . After the third stage success, continue to practise the swinging of the left and right arms. On reaching the top of the wall, your body still lies in midair. At this moment, you will not have any strength to lunge forward. There and then, you should do swinging. Swing your left arm toward the lower-left, and swing your right arm toward the left. With the help of swinging momentum, you will be able to stand at attention on the top of the wall. Left-Form Swing means to swing the right arm first; Right-Form Swing means to swing the left arm first. Now, release the iron-sand, and you will be able to leap onto roofs and vault over walls as quickly and nimbly as an ape (Fig. 68).

Brief Introduction

1. Leaping onto Roofs and Vaulting over Walls Arts, also called " Eight Steps in a Horizontal Row Arts", is one of the soft and internal-strong arts in the seventy-two consummate skills of internal and external Gongfu which the Shaolin Temple has inherited secretly. This is a specific exercise of one's vaulting ability. It is one of the traditional Light-Body Skills.

2. Key to the Exercise; the Shaolin Boxer Master says that it is one of Light-Body Skills and an another method to acquire the leaping-high

Fig. 68

and distant walking ability. It is a secret skill which the Shaolin Wushu inherited. At the beginning, the learner will usually fall down to the ground because of his stiff and inflexible movement. Should the beginner be going all out to make practice, he is sure to master this consummate skill within a measurable length of time.

Frog Arts

Make practice step by step. In the course of practising, guard against impetuousity. For the first step do wrists and arms exercise, which means the upper part body exercise. For the second step do shoulders, chest and abdomen exercises, which means the middle part body exercise. Finally, do legs and buttock exercise, which means the lower part body exercises. All the above exercises cover the techniques of the manipulation of Gong and Energy. i. e. to lay stress on the specific employment of strength instead of only laying stress on the employment of Qi as in the case of Separating Water Arts. In the first step, it is preferable to use a block of stone for exercising the strength of the wrists and arms in the form of Weight Lifting which means to concentrate all strength to all parts of wrists and arms. By and by your strength increases and your muscles will gradually be tougher. Should you be able to make a Weight Lifting of a block of stone of 100 catties, then make an effort to practise directing the energy again, i. e. to clench fists and put the fists down to direct the energy to go to the brain. Then, direct Qi to concentrate energy

248

to the shoulders and arms. Straighten your shoulders backward and energy will travel to all parts of your chest and your back. The result will be
the appearance of the ridged bumps of tough muscles in the upper part of
your body. For the second step of training the midpart of your body, try
to vitalize the energy of the chest and abdomen. This art is similar to that
of the "Iron-Cow Arts" and "Iron-Shirt Arts". After the muscles of the
mid-part of the body become tough, you are to practise the method of applying the energy. After having finished the practice of applying the energy to the muscles of the middle part of the body, you are to make
training of the muscles of the waist and legs of the lower part of the
body. Stand in horse riding stance for several hours. Take a rest while
getting tired. Return to stand in riding-horse stance. The longer, the better. Then strive to practise the method of directing energy. If you can direct the whole energy of your body at your will, the muscles of the lower
parts of your body will become very tough with the appearance of the
swollen bumps of tough muscles (Fig. 69).

Brief Introduction

1. Forg Arts, its another name being "Toad-Rolling Energy Arts", is
commonly called "Raising Stone". This Arts belongs to one of the hard
and external-strong arts in the seventy-two consummate skills of internal
and external Gongfu which the Shaolin Temple has inherited secretly.
Its characteristics belongs to that of "Yang Gang" character. This is a
specific exercise of the body's muscles with the combination of Qigong.

2. The Boxing Proverb says "Inwardly, to master a mouthful of Qi;
Outwardly, to have the bones and skins trained. " It is indispensable to do
exercises in both internal and external organs to have the presence of a

249

Fig. 69

strong figure with high spirit. "Qi" in the Shaolin Proverb refers to both the air breathing and the vital energy of life which travels around inside the body. Enough Qi makes Blood full of life. Only when both Qi and Blood are lively, can your mental and physical strength be strong. "Qi " and " Energy" cooperate each other. " Qi" is the motive power of " Energy" , "Energy " is a manifestation of "Qi". On talking about this respect, Masterhand Monk Jue-Yuan-Shan-Ren, who belonged to Shaolin

250

School, once vividly said that, "Energy becomes Gang (Hardness) from Rou (Softness) and Qi becomes Shi (Solid) through the process of blood circulating and that energy comes from Qi, whereas Qi is hidden (invisible) and energy will be shown. If Qi is not in existence, where does the energy come from? A layman's energy seems to be strong but actually his energy is weak in nature and superficial. The veteran boxer's energy seems to be not worthwhile to be taken care of, but after it approaches or touches an object, it will burst out a formidable amount of energy, as heavy as that of a mountain, which is able to penetrate into the skin and muscles. For this reason, we can see that the layman's power belongs to that of Gang character while the veteran boxer's energy is that of Rou character. Gang is on the surface and Rou, though invisible, can be realistic. One will understand it as time goes on. Therefore, on thrusting out his fist and palm, the Qi rests on three parts of the body: Firstly, it stops on the shoulder, secondly, on the elbows and thirdly, on the palms. It requires much effort for him to exert force throughout to the palm and fingers. With regard to the soft energy, the difference lies, as soon as you raise your hand, that all the energy within the body will travel along with Qi to the part where the Qi circulates. The fact that the Qi is always following the track of the human mentality at a sound speed is believable. "Energy" in the article refers to the speciality of "Toughness" in Shaolin Wushu. It has been a long history that the Shaolin warrior monks have been practising Qigong. The "Inner-Gong Paintings", which the Shaolin Temple inherited, includes a content of seven types. Among them, Twelve-Steps Arts, Inner-Gong Paintings and Twelves Paintings of Changeable Tissus Channels have to do with Qigong. It is clear that the monks in the Shaolin Temple lay emphasis on the combination of

251

Martial Arts and Qigong. Consequently, through the combination of in-ner and outer exercises of "Frog-Arts", "Iron-Shirt Arts" and "Golden-Clock Cover Arts", the Dantian within the body will be filled by Qi, so that the inner Qi current will circulate around the limbs and all or-gans. Not only can you violently attack your opponent, but also you can endure a violent counter-attack. You can bring your skill into full play when combating actually takes place. The poem says, " In the early morning, you relax the limbs for draining waste Qi away. Again and a-gain, you will enjoy good health. Exhaling seems to be a hawk spreying on the fish; Inhaling is just like the roc spreading its wings. At midnight, stick to practing "Wind Sways Willows Arts ". At noon, make every en-deavour to practise Jingan Skill. After dinner, train to have a finger stuck into a piece of metal over and over again. Through the exercise of chopping a hung article , palms' edge will appear to be uneven and rough. Practise head bumping against the bricks with an empty stom-ach. After dinner, practise breaking the stone slabs with raised elbows. Qi flows through Kunglun Acupoint to Jingang Feet. When hungry, one can direct Qi and vault along the wall and walk to a distance of 1000 Li away with cinnabar bound on feet Qi bursted out from Dantian has the force to level the ground. The energy applied to withhold Qi up is compa-rable to a gust of wind suddenly falling the tree down to the ground. -Dantian bursts out Qi which streams into Bai Hui Acupoint. When Qi flows down to Feng-Shi Acupoint, it seems to be drawing a bow. With the "bow" in front, kick with heel leads to assume Pouncing-Tiger Ges-ture. Withhold Qi and make it flow from the heart down to the soles. -With the Qi streaming through legs, you will feel to be riding on horse back, appearing as firm as Taishan with a heaven-ladder being set up.

252

The transformation of Qi into Boxing Skill can be likened to shooting an arrow. It is excellent for its speedy movement.

3. Key to the Exercise; the Shaolin Master says that this Gongfu is an exercise of the muscles for self-defence. To some extent, this Arts is similar to Iron-Shirt Arts. Many people in Tianjin and Tangu in Hebei Province are fond of this skill. It is regretable that the strength training is taken as the dominant factor. This Arts should be regarded as "Inwardly practise the Frog's Qi; Outwardly train the muscle and bones". It is a combination of both an internal and an external exercise and is a means for pursuing longevity.

Iron-Shirt Arts

First, take a belt of soft cloth and bind it to your chest and back for several rounds and then apply force to massage your body. Bend and stretch your elbows and arms again and again like furling the chest to close and open. At night, it's better to sleep on the hard wood board as your bed to let your skeleton touch it. At the start, it may cause unbearable pain. Day by day, your muscles and bones will become tough. Then, set up an iron-pole in front of the house and dig around the pole a shallow sand pit, say, over 1 foot deep. Every morning and evening, strive to practise various skills along the pole. While descending from the pole, try to tumble down against the sands on purpose with shoulders, back, chest, abdomen, arms, and so on. While somersaulting, make the upper part of your body touch the sand twice. Do this type of exercises for three years. Then, remove the soft cloth belt away. Now use a wood hammer to beat your body. Later, use an iron-hammer instead. Now it is time for you to concentrate your mind to direct your Qi to stand the beating. After another three years, training, your upper body will be as pliable

254

as cotton. Now you can be considered to have made success in Iron-Shirt Arts (fig. 70).

Fig. 70

Brief Introduction

1. Iron-Shirt Arts is one of the hard and external-strong arts in the seventy-two consummate skills of internal and external Gongfu which the Shaolin Temple has inherited secretly. It is a specific skill of summoning Qigong to steel the muscles of the body.

2. Key to the Exercise: the Shaolin Master says to the effect that if

this skill and the Inner-Strong Boy Gong are concurrently practised, it is called Golden-Clock Cover Arts, the practice of which definitely requires much effort. Few people can acquire this skill. When you summon your Qi to produce strength, your muscles will become as hard as iron or stone. In the case of fighting, you are unconquerable.

Golden-Clock Cover Arts

First, make a hammer with the waste cloth and beat your whole body. At the start, you may feel painful and from day to day you will gradually feel well. Then, beat with a wood hammer instead. After being beaten with a wood hammer without feeling painful, try to beat with an iron-hammer instead. After having been beaten with an iron-hammer without feeling painful, turn to practise Somersault Arts, Iron-Shirt Arts and Iron-Cow Arts. After two or three years' training, the muscles of your back and your chest will be as hard as iron or stone. Not only can the weapons such as sword or knife hardly hurt you but also the fisting and kicking will not do you any harm (Fig. 71).

Brief Introduction

1. Golden-Clock Cover Arts is one of the hard and external-strong arts in the seventy-two consummate skills of internal and external Gong-fu which the Shaolin Temple has inherited secretly. It belongs to both the Yang Gang character and the inner-strong energy. It is a specific skill of

257

Fig. 71

summoning Qigong to steel the muscles of the body.

2. Key to the Exercise : the Shaolin Master says that this Arts is one of the most important Gongfu in the seventy-two consummate skills. The training method is a little bit complicated. After mastering " Golden-Clock Cover Arts " , the muscles and bones of your chest and your back can be seen to be ridged up and extraordinary tough.

Swimming Skill Arts

In the Swimming Skill, there are eight strokes as follows: Treading, Resisting, Stamping, Floating, Diving, Sinking, Sitting and Plunging. Their styles include: Treading water with the help of feet with the upper body shown, Slanting shoulders to resist water waves, Lifting up Qi to tread water with hands and feet moving, Golden Toad floating on water as rapidly as the wind, Underwater swimming forward, Treading water with hands held high upward, keeping down your Qi to sit on water steadily and diving like dragons fighting against the enemy (Fig. 72).

Brief Introduction

1. Swimming Skill Arts, also called "Waves Diving Arts", "Eight-Step Arts", and "Arts of Diving at the Bottom of Water", is one of the hard and internal-strong arts in the seventy-two consummate skills of internal and external Gongfu which the Shaolin Temple has inherited secretly. This is a specific exercise of the skill on the surface of water.

2. In Shaolin Temple, Master Monk Tong-Chan (the nickname of

259

Fig. 72

Zhu Dechou, an imperial family member in the Ming Dynasty, who took this name after his becoming a monk), once told his disciples as follows: "I made acquaintance with a man who came from Luo Yang city, and whose name was Wu Song-Hou. He was an excellent boxer of the North School. He appeared very strong and would always show his skill in the public. He was specially versed in "Long-Distance Leaping" and could vault over the wall of three or five metres in height as rapidly as

260

an eagle. Once he showed his skill. He asked a man to stand in the middle of a hall. If the man faced the front door, he immediately vaulted over the hall and stood in front of the front door, face to face. If the man turned to face the back door, he could also vault over the hall and stood in front of the back door at once, face to face. He was able to do this for seven or eight times. In fact he could not be said to be unskillful. One day he drank wine with his friend on the riverside. After drinking, they stood and talked on the bank of the river. His friend asked: "Can you leap to the opposite bank?" Wu immediately leaped across the river. His friend asked him to return. Wu leaped back at once. As soon as his feet treaded on the bank, accidently the bank collapsed and he fell into the water. He was drawn into a whirlpool. As he was not a good swimmer, he was unable to leap out of the water to the bankside though he had jumped and leaped up to several feet in height above the surface of the surging waves. Consequently, he was drowned for his being exhausted. " If he were versed in " Swimming Skill", he would not have been drowned. It is thus clear that it is quite necessary to gain mastery in Swimming Skill.

   3. Key to the Exercise: the Shaolin Master says that: " Ability In Swimming" is nowadays called" Swimming Skill". Swimming really has much to do with our daily life. Not only should the boxer master this skill, but an ordinary person must also practise it. In case you travel on boat and happen to come across a storm, you can escape the danger of being drowned if you have the ability to swim. It is necessary for the boxers who live a vagabond life to master the swimming skill.

APPENDIX I :

Shaolin Wushu On Skeleton, Channels And Acupoints

SKULL

The skull consists of the cranium and the mandible. There are eight bones on the left and right. Skull is its general name. In fact, every part of it includes many small bones, nota single one. It has nothing to do with Seizing Skill in Boxing-Here we do not describe it in detail.

SPINAL VERTEBRAE

It is the column of our body, located at the middle of truneal back. It consists of twenty-four small bones. The number of the upper cervical vertebrae is seven; the middle thoracic vertebrae twelve and the lower lumbar vertebrae five. The combination of these three parts is called spinal verterae.

CLAVICULA

Located above the thorax and joints sternum and scapula. Its form is slim and curves and it appears like a key. This bone plays an important function and efficacy in sports and all kinds of work. And it gives assistance to the bones of one's shoulders and arms. It is accessible by seizing skill.

STERNUM

Located at the middle of fore-thorax and between one's two ribs. Counted from the upper 2nd rib to the lower 7th rib. Both of its upper sides joints the clavicula.

SCAPULA

Located above the back of the thorax. One on the right and the other on the left. They are commonly called: "Spoon Bones". Each of its shape is flat with three irregular angles on its three sides. It connects claviculaand humerus and claviada to form a fossa subscapularis at the anterior, which is also called Shoulder-Well. It looks like the wings of a butterfly. Its anterior and posterior bones are accessible by seizing skill.

HUMERUS

It is a long tubular bone. Its ball-shaped superior extremity joints the scapula. Its flat-shaped inferior extremity joints the anterior limb bone. The upper part of the corpus humeri is cylindrical and the lower part is triangular. There is a tuber at the lateral and a slender sulcus at the middle. The right and left bones are accessible by seizing skill.

RADIUS

It is a part of the anterior limb bone and a tubular bone of the trigonal shape. Its upper part is oval. There is a trigonal articulatio at the inferior extremity where it joints the bone of one's hand. It is located at the lateral to anterior limb bone. It is bigger than ulna. And it joints the upper limb bone and ulna. It is easily accessible by seizing skill.

263

ULNA

It joints the radius and forms a part of anterior limb bone. It is also a trigonal tubular bone like humerus and radius. Its upper part is big and its lower part is semi-circle. It is located in the middle between the anterior limb bone and the ulna bone to form a narrow and long gap. It is easy for one to seize it from the left or right.

OSSA CARPI

It's also known as radicular bone of one's hand and is between anterior limb bone and ossa metacarpi. It consists of eight bones, including os naviculave manus, os lunatum, os triquetrum, os pisiforme, os multangulum matum, os mnitangulum minus, os capitatum and os hamatum. - Their shapes are rather short and they joint each other and cannot act individually. If one of them moves, the rest will follow. It is a key point in the case of the practice of seizing skill.

BONE OF HAND

It is divided into ossa metacarpi and ossa digitorum manus and its general name is called Bone Of Hand. Ossa metacarp is located between ossa carpi and ossa digitorum manus. It is five in all and called: lst ossa metacarpi, 2nd ossa metacarpi ......, according to the number in order, The lst one is the shortest and very thick; the 2nd one is the longest and slimmer than the first one. The rest of them is somewhat different. Ossa digitorum manus, which is located at the anterior extremity of the ossa metacarpi, is also called according to number in order, i. e. the lst ossa metaearpi, the 2nd ossa metacarpi···, Ossa metacarpi is consisted of four-

264

teen small bones in all. Only the first one is of two segments, Four of the rest are of three segments. There are articulatios which takes charge of the motion of all bone joints. It is easy for one to seize it from the left or right.

PELVIS

Located at the lower part of one's trunk. As it looks like a plate, it is called "Plate Bone" (Pan Gu). It joints one's thigh. Of male, the bone is narrow and long; Of female, it's wide and short. It is not useful for boxers in fighting. Here we do not describe it in detail.

STERNUM

It's flat and oblong. The upper part is wide and thick, and it is named Handle. Sternum is that of counting from the second os costae to the seventh. The middle is corpus sternum; the lower is processue xiphoideus. It faces the spinal vertebrae. Avoid seizing it.

OS COSTAE

It protects the upper part of our body and has twelve pairs on the left and right in all. The upper seven pairs connect with sternum and they are named "Real Os Costae". The lower five pairs don't connect with sternum and are called "False Os Costae". Although their upper three pairs don't connect with sternum, they joint the upper costal carti- lage. The lower two pairs, of which its left and right are opposite, don't joint anywhere, are located at the lower part of sternum separately and are called Floating Os Costae, for they seem to be floating. They are not suitable for the practice of seizing skill because they are crisp and break

265

easily.

VERTEBRAE LUMBALES

This is a general name for the lower five bones of the spinal vertebrae. Please refer to the Spinal Vertebrae. It is not suitable for the practice of seizing skill.

OS SACRUM

Located below the vertebrae lumbales. It is consisted of five small
bones closely and never move. It is crisp. It is not suitable for the boxers
to make practice of seizing skill.

ACETABULUM

Acetabulum is a forea of the bone and joints the articulation. It is
located on two sides of the pevis, i. e. the lateral sides of os coxae. Its
fovea is very deep and resembles a cupping for holding the superior extremity of the thigh. Acetabulum joints the superior extremity of the
thigh and connects with cartilage to form a artiallatio of the thigh, It is
an important part of our body. Its function is the same as that of the articulatio human. Only its external cartilage is thicker. It can control the
motion of one's leg. It is suitable for the boxers to make practice of seizing skill.

FEMUR

Located at the lower of os coxar's lateral. Its superior extremity
connects with the acetabulum and its inferior extremity with the patella
and tibia. It is the largest tubular bone of our body. Where the superior

266

extremity joints the os coxae looks like a ball. The middle part is some-what triangular; the inferior extremity is projecting round. One of the inferior extremities connects with patalla; the other connects with tibia. The articulatio of femur plays an important role in the seizing skill.

PATELLA

Located at the centre of femour's inferior extremity, that is to say, it joints the femour's posterior articular surface. So the patella is in the middle between the femour and tibia. It is a covering instrument of the joints of one's two bones, and is called"Knee". These joints in all actually take charge of the movement of femour abd tibia. It plays an important role in the seizing skill.

FIBULA

Located at the lateral of the shank and in a parallel with the tibia sick. Its superior extremity does not directly connect with the thigh and patella, it lies by the side of the inferior of condylus lateralis on the junction of the superior extremity of tibia and femour. The projecting malleolus lateralis of the inferior extremity contact with the talus. The superior extremity of the fibula is square and its middle is trigonal while the inferior extremity is flat triangle. It helps tibia to support a part of shank and is also quite important for the practice of seizing skill.

TIBIA

Located in the middle of the shank and in parallel with the fibula. The superior extremity closely joints the inferior extremity of the thigh, and its anterior surface connects with the patella. The tibia is a tubular bone, too, and is much larger than the fibula. The superior extremity of the tibia is a flat triangule. The middle is cylindrical. The inferior extremity is square and joints talus. There is a narrow and long crevice between the tibia and talus, it is the most suitable for one to make practice of seizing skill.

OSSA TARSI

It's also called "Bone of Heel". Located at the lower part of the tibia and fibula. It consists of the talus, calcaneus, os narviallare pedis, os cuneiforme, and os cuboideum to form the heel and joints various parts of the shank. Ossa Tarsi's inferior surface connects with ossa metatarsi. In fact, it is located between the shank and ossa metatarsi. It is similar to the upper ossa carpi but the shape of jointing is somewhat different. This articulation is a most gristly organ. Once it is being slightly shaken, it will be injured or dislocated. As its position is rather small, it is also suitable for one to make practice of seizing skill.

OSSA METATARSI AND DIGITORUMPEDIS

Located between the ossa tarsi and ossa digitorumpedis. Its posterior extremity connects with tarsi; the anterior with ossa digitorumpedis and its number is five. According to the number in order, it's called: the 1st ossa metatarsi, the 2nd ossa metatarsi. This bone is cylindrical, the 1st is the shortest, the 2nd is the longest. Ossa digitorumpedis is named for its means of number, and is fourteen in all. Only 1st ossa digitorumpedis (i. e. big digitorumpedis) splits into two segments, the rest four bones are three segments each being the smallest part of bones. There exist many articulatios. Even if they are seized they won't suffer much.

268

RISORIUS TENDON AND MUSCLE

It belongs to one of the face's tendon. Two sides of the angulus oris are separately divided into three tendons. It takes charge of the movement of the mouth. One of them holds responsible for the Smile and is called Risorius Tendon And Muscle. On the face, besides it links to the other parts of the muscle, the tendon properly indicates the happiness, anger, sadness and delight. In the seizing art, not only can the tendons on the chest and back be put into use, but also the rest of tendons can be brought into full play.

EAR TENDON

It consists of all sorts of Helix Tendons, the shape of which is very small and the ability of which is very weak. And it can not move itself. But, in the case of the animals f. i. the rabbits, dogs, horses and mules, their ears are large and can move themselves. They differs from those of the mankind. All parts of the ear, for instance, Mitroid Tendon, Retroauricular Tendon, Sternocleidomastoideus Tendon, etc. certainly have something to do with the brain. Among the channels, it takes the vital position, too. In the Boxing Skill, Helix Tendon has nothing to do with it, but if one's retroaurilar is caught heavily, not only will he be defeated, but also he may suffer from fainting or even death.

FLECTION TENDON

Whatever one's limbs do freely depends on the function of his supporting skeletons and the shrinking and contracting of his joints and the activities of channels as well. This so-called Flection Tendon is the most

269

important factor. This tendon exists in all joints and is not confined to any part of one's body. Although each of them has its different names for its different positions, it can still be called Flection Tendon. Their positions are respectively on the inner-sides of all limbs joints. If one strectches his tendons, his limbs will be straight If one shrinks his tendons his limbs will curve. If one's flection tendon is seized, it will strongly contract. The part with its Flection Tendon being seized will not be able to be stretched and one will lose his ability of movement. Hence he will be defeated. Therefore, wherever it lies, it is the most important part in the Boxing Skill to be taken care of.

EXTENSION TENDON

Its position and function are quite different from those of the flection tendon. It can not be neglected. Each extension tendon has its different name for its different positions. It is located on the outer-side of joints. If one strecthes it, his limbs will shrink. If one shrinks it, his limbs will be straight. If it is seized, it will strongly contract and the part which has been seized doesn't bend. Thus one can neither stretch nor shrink at ease and he will lose his ability of resistent ability. So it is an important part of one's body, too.

TENDON ABDOMEN

The tendon of a human body can be divided into three parts: Head, Abdomen, Tail. The Tendon Abdomen is very soft and smooth, just like the silks, but it is very tensile and it has different shapes, slim or long, thick or short, thin or flat due to its position. However its function is the same. It adheres to the bones or between junctures and depends on the

270

tendon abdomen energy to pull or draw each other. We can find this kind of tendon in the pork. If it is injured, one's bones and muscles may be out of their proper positions. Its effects can not be neglected. It is very important in the Boxing Skill.

TENDON TAIL

Tendon Head and Tendon Tail have their different shapes. Unlike the tendon abdomen, the functions of the tendon tail are those of covering the bones and preventing them from injury. Although it is different from the tendon abdomen, it has the same function of protecting ability. As all organs of a human body have their respective excellent functions and can not be lacked the Tendon Tael is dispensable too especially in the case of practising the seizing skill.

TENDON MEMBRANE

It is a vital medium for connecting two tendons or many tendons. The tendon membrane lies between the tendons for separating them to prevent them from congesting into a mess. It is white and thin. We can find them in the pork mutton or beef . Although it is the vital and indespensible part of the body, it has nothing to do with the Boxing Skill, for it can not be easily found. And in the event of its being seriously injured, the whole body may not be effected.

SURAL TENDON

It is a very important tendon in the Seizing Skill. It is also the vital tenson of one's heels. The structure of one's knee-joints differs from that of the other bones. It takes charge of the movement of one's thigh and shank. It is the main tendon of the knees' joints and the juncture of one's thigh bones, knee bones and tibial bones. Its position sets on the outer-side of the knee and is called Outer-Sural Tendon. And its position on the centre of one's upper knee is called Middle-Sural Tendon. All activities of one's legs and tibial depend on this tendon. If it is injured, the lower part of one's leg will lose its ability and one can not stand or walk. It is not very big but it's easy to be caught in the case of combating.

TAIYANG ACUPOINT(Sun Acupoint)

Located on both sides of the forehead, the left being Tai Yang and the right Tai Yin. Nowadays it is generally called Taiyang Acupoint being a vital part of the head. It is "Dead Acupoint" among the twenty-four Acupoints. One will be faint or even die if it is slightly seized .

TAINRONG ACUPOINT

Located on the back of ears and is in parallel with the ear. It lies on the outer-side of Fen Yi Acupoint, and is above the Tian Chuang acupoint. It is vital acupoint of the back of one's head. It is also a "Dead Acupoint" among the twenty-four acupoints.

FENGFU ACUPOINT

Located in the centre of the low part of one's back head and is below the Naohu Acupoint but above the Yamen Acupoint. It's in parallel with the left and right FenYi Acupoint. It is a single Acupoint. It is a vital part of one's back brain. It is a "Dead Acupoint" , too. If this acupoint is seized, one may faint or die immediately.

272

TIANZHU ACUPOINT

Located on either side of the Yamen Acupoint and lies below the zhen acupoint. It is a "Dead Acupoint" among the twenty-four acupoints. If it is seized, one may faint or die at once.

LIANQUAN(Corner Fountain)ACUPOINT

Located in the middle above the Adam's apple and is in the depression at the upper border of the hyoid bone. It is also in the middle position of one's neck. It is one of the "Dead Acupoint". If it is seized, one may die immediately.

JIANJING(Shoulder Well)ACUPOINT

Located on the inner-side of the shoulder-tip between the scapula and clavicle. It is also called JianWo(Shoulder Cave). It lies below the Jianchong Acupoint. There are two such acupoints on the outer-sides of Tiandin Acupoints. Although it's not "Dead Acupoint", one will feel forceless and his limbs can not move at all if either of them is seized.

JUGU (Great Bone)ACUPOINT

Located on the outer-side of Jianjing acupoint. There are two. Each of them lies in the centre of the shoulder-tip, i. e. the juncture of the shoulder bone and the arm bone. It is one of the Areolar Acupoints among the twenty-four acupoints. It is inferior to the Jianjing Acupoint.

BINAO (Median Dide Of Upper Arm) ACUPOINT

Located below the Jugu Acupoint and in the centre of the upper postarm i. e. between the Nuhui and Tianquan acupoint. It is a vital acupoint of one's postarm. They are two with either of them on the left or on the right side. It belongs to Ren Ma Acupoint in the skill of pressing acupoints. It is called Areolar Acupoint. If it is seized, one will fall down to the ground for his tingling feeling.

WULI (Five Li) ACUPOINT

Located below the Binao and above the elbow. It is a vital part of one's upper postarm, too. They are two with either of them on the left or on the right. If it is seized, one will lose his ability of movement.

QUCHI (Pool Bend) ACUPOINT

When the elbow is flexed, the point is in the depression of the lateral end of the transverse cubital crease, i. e. midpoint between Chize and the lateral epicondyle of the humerus. It is a vital part of one's arms. Although it is not a "Dead Acupoint", it is also an important point.

SHAOHAI (Shaoyin Sea) ACUPOINT

Its location is just contrary to that of the Quchi. It lies on the inner-side of the elbow joint, i. e. the juncture of postarm bones and forearm bones. If the arm is stretched, there exists a sinking pit on the inner-side of one's arm. Shaohai Point just locates in the centre of this pit. They are two with either of them on the left or on the right. It plays an important role in the process of learning the Pressing Acupoint.

QUZE (Marsh On Bend) ACUPOINT

Located on the upper part of one's forearms and below the Chizhe

274

acupoint. It lies between the Shaohai and Shanli acupoints. In the Pressing Acupoint it is a Areolar Acupoint too. Although it is not a channel , it is very sensitive to the seizing skill.

YANCHI ACUPOINT

Located at the juncture of one's wrist and forearm bones and in the upper-rear of one's Tiger-Mouth i. e. the inner-side of the back of one's palms. The upper is Pianli Acupoint and the lower is Hegu Acupoint. They are two with one on either side. It plays an important role in the wrists and arms. It is one of the Pressing Acupoints. Its effect is not inferior to that of Quchi.

YANGU ACUPOINT

Located on the juncture of one's wrist and forearm on the back of the hand, but its location is contrary to that of Yanchi Acupoint. They are in parallel with each other. They are important organs in the Areolar Acupoint.

MAIWAN ACUPOINT

Located in the front of one's wrist, forearm of upper wrist-joint, near to the thumb, in the depression of the juncture of ulna and radius. It is commonly called Maimen (The Pulse Door) the place where the traditional Chinese doctor feel the pulse of one's body, and takes an important position of one's wrist. If it is seized, one may fall down to the ground. If it is seized for too long time, one may die. It is one of Dead Acupoints.

QIMEN ACUPOINT

Located on the mammillary line, two ribs below the nipple, in the 6th intercostal space. If it is seized, it can also cause somebody to suffer from death.

ZHANMENG ACUPOINT

Located below the Qimen Acupoint, above the front waist, at the end of the rib and opposite to the back Jinchu Acupoint. It is divided into the left and right Zhanmeng. It is a "Dead Acupoint" too. If it is seized heavily, one may die at once.

FENGWEI ACUPOINT

Located at the back of the body above Jinchu Acupoint and on the outer-side of the back. They are two with one on either side, opposite to the Qimen Acupoint, and in parallel with the Jixing Acupoint. It is one of the large points among the Areolar Acupoint. If it is seized or pressed heavily for a little while, one may fall down immediately or his internal organs will be injured.

JINCHU ACUPOINT

Located right under the Fengwei Acupoint, above the waist. They are two with one on either side. Their positions are the same as those of the Fengwei Acupoint, but different in their location. If it is seized heavily, one may not die at once, but can not live long. However, his life can be saved with the medicinal treatment.

276

BAIHAI (White Sea) ACUPOINT

Its location is on the inner-side of the thigh and opposite to the Huang Tiao Acupoint. There are two with one on the left and the other on the right. It occupies a vital position of one's leg. It is the biggest areolar acupoint. But it is not easy to be seized for its thick muscle. Without strong force, one can not get an access to it.

WEIZHONG ACUPOINT

Midpoint of transverse crease of the popliteal fossa, between the tendons of muscle biceps femoris and semitendinosus. Locate the point in prone position or with flexed knee. It is one of the Areolar Point among the seizing points. For its thin muscle, it is easy for one to seize it. And one need not overexert force but the time must be proper. One will be faint if he is being seized.

CHUPIN ACUPOINT

Located on the inner-side of one's shank, at the midpoint between the fibula and tibia and above the Jiaoxing Acupoint. Its muscle is full and projecting. It is commonly called Yellow Fish Abdomen. It is one of the Areolar Acupoint among the twenty-four acupoints. Although its muscle is not as thick as that of white Sea Acupoint, it is much more thicker than that of the Weizhong Acupoint. To seize this acupoint one is to exert stronger force to do it or he will get little result.

KUNGSUN (Luo-Connecting Point) ACUPOINT

Located in the leg, i. e. in the juncture of ankle bones and tibia

277

i. e. the lower position of the inner-side of the ankle bones, at the back of Dazhuang Acupoint. They are a pair with one on either side. It is one of the main point of one's leg and is an areolar acupoint, too. If it is seized, one will be unable to stand up for its soft bones are suffering from tingling feeling.

YONHQUAN (GUSH SPRING) ACUPOINT

In the depression appearing on the sole when the foot is in plantar flexion, approximately at the juncture of the anterior and middle third of the sole. If it's being seized, one may die at once. It is one of the main" Dead Acupoints".

*   *   *

In the above-mentioned twenty-four acupoints, there lie both Dead and Areolar Acupoints. If it is not out of absolute necessity, one never seizes his opponent's Dead Point.

Shaolin Temple Secret Recipe On Rescuing

Main Prescription to Treat Internal and/or External wounds(add or deduct according to the seriousness of an individual case.)

Chinese Angelica, Chuanxiong Rihizome, Dried Rehmania Root, Dipsacus Root, 2 qian each. Sappan Wood (get rid of oil), Myrrh (get rid of oil), Akebia Stem, Lindero Root, Herb Of Hirsute Shing, 1 qian each. Bugleweed Peach (get rid of skin and tip) fourteen grains. Liguorice Root, eight fen. Costusroot, eight fen. Fresh Ginger, three tablets. And, add a cup of Baby's Urine and a cup of Rice Wine. (Note: 1 fen = 0. 5 gram; 1 qian = 5 grams; 1 tael = 50 gram)

After prescribing an added ingredient leading the efficacy of the above prescribed main medicines through the main channel or channels, should the following symtoms appeared add as follow.

Blood Stasis and Chest Coagulation; add Ambmum Fruit, 1 qian and 5 fen.

Heart Attacking Heart and Qi Tends to Exhaust; add Lighter Salt Fevmented Soybean, 1 qian.

Qi Attacking Heart; add Clove, 1 qian.

Dyspnea; add Bitter Apricot Rernel, Bitter Orange 1 qian each.

Ravings; add Ginseng, 1 qian. Chinnabar, 5 fen. with the silver ware and gold ware decocted together.

Aphonia: add Costus Root, Calamus Rhizome, 1 qian each.

Obstruction of Air Passage: add Magnolia Bark, and Gentian Root, 1 qian each. Tangenne Pee, 5 fen.

Fever: add Bupleurum, Scutellaria Root, White Peony Root, Peppermint, Ledebouriella, 1 qian each. Herb of Manchurian, 5 fen.

Blood Stasis: add Fa Hui (Hair Ash), 2 qian.

Forced Laughing: add Cattail Pollen qian, Sichuan Chinabery, 2 qian.

Waist Injured: Po Gu Zhi, Eacommia Bark, 1 qian each. Bark of Chinese Cassia Tree, Fennel, 8 fen each.

Constipation: add Rhubarb, Chinese Angelica, 2 qian each. Pu Xiao, 1 qian.

Dyuria: add Herb Of Fineleat Schizomepeta, Rhubarb, Herb Of Lilac Pink, 1 qian each. Bitter Apricot Rernel (get rid of skin and tip), fourteen grains.

Hematuria: add Sichan Chinabery, 1 qian. Biota Top, 2 qian.

Urethremorrhage: add Pomegranate Rool 1 qian and 5 fen Flower of Garden Eggplant, 2 qian.

Constipation and Bradyuria: add Rhubarb, Bitter Apricot Rernel, Bark of Chinese Cassia Tree, 1 qian and 5 fen each

Incontinence of Urine: add Bark of Chinese Cassia Tree, Clove, 1 qian each.

Fecal Incontinence: add Cimicifuge Rhizome, Astragalus Root, Chebnla Fruit, Platycodon, 1 qian each.

Enterodynia and Cold Feeling: add Yanhusuo, Rhizome of Lessor Galangal, 1 qian each.

280

Cough: add Don Key-hide Gelatin, 2 qian. Seed of Tuber Onion, one cup.

Slight Enterodynia on the Left: add Caoguo, Capsule Of Weeping Forsythia, Dahurian Angeliea Root, 1 qian each.

Prolapse of Rectum: add Cimicifuga Rhizome, Bupleurum Root, Astragalus Root, Bighead Atractylodes Rhizome, 1 qian each. Tangenne Pee, Liquorice, 5 fen each.

Slight Enterodgnia on the Right: add Foeniculum Vulgare Mill, Indian Bread, 1 qian each. Chinese Onion three pieces.

Hemoptysis: add cattail Pollen, Rubus Parri Folius, 1 qian each.

Stool from the Mouth: add clove, Tsaoko, Tackin thepulpit Tuber of pinellia, 1 qian each. Fruit of Cocklebur-like Amomum, Seven grains.

Slurred Speech Caused By Shortened Tongue: add Ginseny, Coptis Root, Gypsum, 1 qian each.

Lengthen Tongue About One Inch: add Fresh Batryticated Silkworm, Furnace Soil, 1 qian each, Raw Iron, 4 taels and Rice Bean, about one hundred grains.

Veside of Tongue: add Peppermint, 2 qian. Fresh Ginger, 1 qian.

Ear Polyp: add Salt Fermented So-ybean, 1 qian.

Hiccup: add Bupleurum Root, Root-Bark of Slender-style Acanthopanax, Furit of Common Floweringquince, Plantain Seed, 1 qian each.

Nine Orifices Bleeding: add Seed of Cochinchina, Momordica, Bark of Chinese Redbud, 1 qian each. A cup of Babys Urine.

Lumbago Can't Turn To Sides: add three cup of thick tea, and a cups of Aged Rice Wine.

General Pain, Turn to both sides with difficulty: add Morinda

Root, Achyranthes, Cassia Ywig, Eacommia Bark, 1 qian each.

Swollen: add Ledebouriella, Herb Of Fineleaf Schizomepeta, White Peony Root, 1 qian each.

Throat Dry and Vomiting While Taking Drugs: put sweetened bean paste on the tongue for half an hour and swallow it with the drug.

Throat Dryless and Vomiting While Taking Drug: add Nutgrass Flatsedge Rhizome, Ambmum Fruit, Clove, 1 qian each.

Speech Rhembasmus and from Time to Time in Lethargic State: add Costusroot, Cinnabar, Borax, Amber, 1 qian each. Root of Tibet Gentian, 5 qian.

Reflux of Blood and Qi Attacking Heart: use a pair of Black-Bone Silky Rowl and add the Rice Wine. A Little Black Bean Juice Take Them with drug.

Headache Like Cracking: add Desertliring Cistanche, Dahurian Angeliea Root, 1 qian each.

Heart-Sick: add Dahurian Angeliea Root, Bark of Officinal Magnolla, Ligusticum Root, Scutellaria Root, 1 qian each.

Eye Injured: add Cassia Reed, half a qian. Fruit Of simpleleaf Shrub Chasteree, 4 fen.

Nose Injured: add Magnolia Flower, Turtle Shell, 1 qian each.

Laryn (Throat)Injured: add Green Fish Gall, Algefacient Powder.

Cheeks Injured: add Pubescent Angelica Root, Herb of Manchurian, 1 qian each.

Lip Injured: add Cimicifuge Rhizome, Root Of Largeleaf Gentian, Achyranthes, 1 qian each.

Teeth Injured: add Flower Of Pmerger Pipewort, 1 qian.

Teeth Shaking: add Bubescent Angelica Root, 1 qian. Herb of

282

Manchurian, 7 fen. In addition to this, use Chinese Nut-Gall, Earthwormh, Dusting Powder Root Of Tooth for treatment.

Left Shoulder Injured: add Green Tangerine Peel, 1 qian 5 fen.

Right Shoulder Injured: add Cimicifuga Rhizome, 1 qian and 5 fen. If there exists the other wounds on the body, it can be taken.

Hand Injured: add Cassia Twig, Limonite, 1 qian each. Ginger Decoction, three spoons.

Breast Injured: add Lily Bubb, Fritillary, Root of Uniflower Swisscentaury, 1 qian each.

Chest Injured: add Bupleurum Root, Bitter Orange, 1 qian each. A cup of Seed Of Tuber Onion

Left Hypochondrium Injured: add White Mustard Seed, Bupleurum Root, 1 qian each.

Right Hypochondrium Injured: add Broom Cypress Fruit, White Mustard Seed, Astragalus Root, 1 qian each, Cimicifuge Rhizome, 1 fen.

Stomach Injured: add Shell of Aveca Nut, 1 qian.

Back Injured: add Amomum Fruit, Costusroot, 1 qian each.

Waist Injured: add Eacommia Bark, Po Gu Zhi, 1 qian each.

Waist and Hypochondrium Pain: add Garden Balsant Seed, 2 qian.

Abdomen Injured: add Fennel, Garden Balsant Seed 1 qian each.

Out-Kedney Injured And Suffering From Retention of Urine: add musk, 2 fen. Camphor, 3 fen. A Cup of Lettuce Seed. To grind these three sorts of drugs into fine powder and pound the lettuce leaf into an adhesive plaster, and mix with the drug and paste it on the navel.

Anus Injured: add Areca Seed, Japanese Pogodatree, Rhubard of Parch, 1 qian each

Legs Injured: add Achyranthes, Fruit of Common Flower, In-

283

gquince, Dendrobium Root Bark of Slenderstyle Acanthopanax, Perilla Stem, 1 qian each.

Heels Injured: add Foeniculum Vulgare Mill, Bark of Chinese Redbud, Sappan Wood, 1 qian each.

Bones Injured: add Fruit of Siberian Cocklebur, Rhizome 〖f Fortune's Drynaria, 1 qian each.

Joints Injured: add Fushen, Bighead Atractylodes Rhizome, 2 qian each.

Swelling and Pain: add Ginseny, Prepared Daughter Root of Common Monkhood, 1 qian each.

Blood Statis and Swelling and Pain: choose the Tian Yin Acupoint and prick it bleeding with silver needle.

Swelling and Pain, Fever Cause Anorexia: add Ginseny, Astragalus Root, Rhizome Of Largehead Atractylodes, Bupleurum, 1 qian each.

Fever and Pain Between 3 and 7 in the Morning: add Tangerine Pee, 5 fen. Astragalus Root, Rhizome of Largehead Atractylodes, 1 qian each. Coptis Root, 8 fen.

Swelling and Pain but Not Red: add Po Gu Zhi, Star Anise, Morinda Root, 1 qian each, Dodder Seed, 1 qian and 5 fen.

Swelling but Not Pain: add Red Peony Root, Prepared Rhizome of Rehmannia, Eacommia Bark, Rhizome of Swordlike Atractylodes, 1 qian each.

Swelling, Moisture Frigidity and Fever: add Hawthorn Fruit, Rhizome of Common Yam, Magnolia Bark, Bighead Atractylodes Rhizome, 1 qian each. Amomum Fruit, 7 grains.

Swelling, Yellow Face and Fever: add Ginseny, Astragalus Root, 7 fen. Bighead Atractylodes Rhizome, Cimicifuge Rhizome, 1 fen each.

284

Tangerine Pee , 8 fen.

—— Extract from "Secret Recipe On Rescuing"

少林武术秘传绝技 72 功法

吴佳明　编　　柔刚　译

福建科学技术出版社出版

（中国福建福州市得贵巷 27 号）

邮政编码 350001

福建省地质测绘制印厂排版印刷

中国国际图书贸易总公司发行

（中国北京车公庄西路 35 号）

北京邮政信箱第 399 号　邮政编码 100044

1992 年(大 32 开)第一版

（英）

ISBN 7　5335—0486—0/G · 67(外)

00810

7-E-2706P